Eric Hosking's Birds

Eric Hosking's Birds

Fifty Years of Photographing Wildlife

Eric Hosking

with Kevin MacDonnell

Foreword by Roger Tory Peterson

Pelham Books
London

First published in Great Britain by PELHAM BOOKS LTD,
44-45 Bedford Square, WC1 1979.

Copyright © 1979 Walter Parrish International Limited

ISBN 0 7207 1163 0

Designed and produced by Walter Parrish International Limited, London.

Printed and bound in Hong Kong by Leefung-Asco Printers Limited.

Contents

To the memory of my mother
and father who understood
my love of birds.

Preface

This book was initially the brainchild of my son David who, unknown to me and while I was abroad, took the idea to Walter Parrish International. They showed considerable enthusiasm and I have not had a minute's peace since! The idea was to celebrate three anniversaries falling in 1979 – fifty years as a professional wildlife photographer, seventy years of age and forty years of very happy marriage.

This is primarily a picture book, its purpose to show a selection of some of my better photographs. The text is intended to be incidental, covering the circumstances in which many of the pictures were taken, some photographic technicalities, some of the interesting features of the birds photographed, and in the case of three of the chapters accounts of photographic expeditions in foreign places.

My life has been devoted to photography, not to writing, and without the help of Kevin MacDonnell it is doubtful whether there would have been any text. I am very grateful to him not only for knocking my thoughts and ideas into shape but also for putting so much of his own work on one side to get it completed in time.

In the production of a book of this nature there has been a host of people who have given invaluable aid. I would like to acknowledge them all but to do so would make a long and meaningless list. However, there are a few who have done so much their names must be included.

Most important is my wife Dorothy, who helped me with so many ideas, particularly in getting chapters started and rounded off so that all I had to do was fill in the middle bit. But apart from this we have had so many all-day meetings at our home with Walter Parrish International when she provided mountains of sandwiches and gallons of coffee. When I was practically crawling up the wall with everything that had to be done, she calmed me down and kept me on an even keel.

David, our younger son who is now in partnership with me, has coped with most of the business so that I could spend as much time as possible on this book. He has also helped me with ideas and supplied some of the photographs reproduced in this book in which he has used the very latest photographic methods, a few of which are still being developed.

My grateful thanks are due to Dr Roger Tory Peterson, the finest ornithologist, naturalist and artist living today, for his kindly reminiscent Foreword. When Dorothy and I made our first visit to the United States in 1962 we arrived at Kennedy Airport at six o'clock in the morning and there to meet us was Roger, who must have got up at the crack of dawn to drive from his home in Connecticut – this surely is the sign of a true friend.

Although most of the photographs are of birds in a free and wild state I have done a certain amount of work at some of the zoos. I would especially like to record my thanks to Chester Zoo, whose founder, George Mottershead, took so much interest in my work right up to the time of his death. His successor, Dr Michael Brambell, has very kindly agreed to my continuing to take photographs and I owe a lot to both Bill Timmis and Peter Bloomfield, who have assisted me so well. Len Hill of Birdland, Bourton-on-the-Water, has often gone to a great deal of trouble to provide birds for me to portray and has also had us to stay with him. Bernard Sayers, of Chelmsford, has a wonderful collection of owls and some of the pictures in this book are of his birds. It was his fine specimen of an Eagle Owl that put on the dramatic aggressive display that resulted in the double-page picture on pages 40-1.

David and I cannot express sufficiently our thanks to Phillip Glasier and his family who made us so welcome at the Falconry Centre in Newent. His birds have been a real joy to photograph. As I write this, David and Phillip have just succeeded in getting a superb shot of a Lanner Falcon, travelling at some 60 miles per hour, taken with the new high-speed flash and photo-electric shutter release.

Some members of the British Trust for Ornithology, especially Tom Kittle, have given us a lot of help, not only in providing subjects but also in making valuable suggestions for the improvement of our equipment. We are deeply indebted to Professor John Craggs of the Department of Electrical Engineering and Electronics at the University of Liverpool, and particularly to Paul Watkinson, who devised and built our new high-speed flash set with which we have taken some of the birds in flight.

John Chesshyre and Clare Howell, both of Walter Parrish International, have been extremely helpful, the former with the writing, editing and captioning, the latter with the selection of the pictures. We have over 90,000 colour transparencies and some 250,000 black and white pictures of about 1800 species of birds, as well as mammals, reptiles, amphibians, fish, flowers and trees, and Clare has been through most of them.

Lastly, I must fend off my critics by emphasizing that the title of the British edition was chosen by my publishers, not by me. 'Eric Hosking's Birds' sounds terribly conceited to me. The birds are certainly not mine. I have obtained so much enjoyment from watching and photographing them and I hope that my readers will have the pleasure of doing the same, and so find a new wonder and beauty in the natural world around them.

Foreword

When the late James Fisher introduced me to Eric Hosking I felt an immediate rapport with this open, friendly man. His passion for birds was something I could understand. He was in his early forties, just a year younger than I, and even less travelled. I had only recently broken the bonds of provincialism by crossing the Atlantic to attend my first International Ornithological Congress. It was on my return to England in 1952 to work intensively with Guy Mountfort and Phil Hollom on the *Field Guide to the Birds of Britain and Europe* that Eric Hosking and I became firm friends.

In October, just before I returned home after eight or nine months in London, it was my good fortune to spend a week on Hilbre Island off the west coast of England with Eric and the little group of photographers who made a holiday of it twice a year at the time of the highest tides when thousands of Oystercatchers, Knots, Dunlins and other waders are crowded onto Hilbre's satellite islands, the 'Big Eye' and the 'Little Eye'. A hide properly placed is almost sure to be surrounded by countless waders at high tide – a photographic spectacle. It was because of Eric that I managed to crash this exclusive party. Others had hopefully placed their names on the list for two or three years, but at the last moment there was accommodation for just one guest. I was the lucky one who joined Eric, Bill Wilson, Norman Ellison of the BBC, Ronnie Pryor, Joe Wells, Jerry Jamieson, Dr McAfee and, most glamorous of all, Field Marshal the Viscount Alanbrooke. As one would expect of a military man, Lord Alanbrooke brought along his heavy artillery – a 14″ lens mounted on a 16mm Kodak Ciné-Special. This was his seventh visit to Hilbre. Even Prince Philip had joined in the fun on occasions.

Each day we put up our hides at least two hours before the tide came in. I might say that I had never seen any hide quite as effective or well made as a Hosking hide; unless it was the one Lord Alanbrooke had which was an adaptation of the same design. Lord Alanbrooke let me work from his hide one morning. It had everything except hot and cold running water.

I would not dare estimate the numbers of Oystercatchers that crowded the eroded red sandstone of the Little Eye. At first there were a few dozen, then hundreds, then thousands. Closer and closer they crowded, kleeping, and making an incredible racket while the build-up continued. At the very moment of high tide a silence suddenly fell over the assembly and every last bird tucked its long orange bill into the feathers of its back and went to sleep. So busy had I been photographing the spectacular Oystercatchers out of one side of my hide that I was quite unaware of what had been taking place on the other. Hearing a sudden rush of wings, I peeped out. There, just a few feet away, was a great grey carpet of Knots. There were thousands. More were dropping in and so crowded were they that some stood on the backs of others. I was told that sometimes the Knots exceed 50,000 in a single flock – a nation of Knots. Like an international army on review, each species tended to maintain its own ranks. The Redshanks gathered by the hundreds on certain rocks, the Turnstones on others.

While we were preparing shrimp and mussels for the evening meal Eric told me that it was his goal to film every British bird and for that reason he felt no great urge to travel outside Britain. 'But,' I asked, 'what of those accidental strays that have crossed the Channel or the open sea to find a place on the British list?' He admitted that he had recently taken the boat ferry to nearby Holland to photograph Spoonbills and Avocets, birds that formerly nested in England.

It was Guy Mountfort who finally weaned Eric from his exclusive involvement with the birds of his mother country. 'There is a geat big world out there, Eric,' said Guy. 'Perhaps you should see some of it. Would you care to join a group of us in Spain for a month in the Marismas? Lord and Lady Alanbrooke will be going. So will James Fisher, James Ferguson-Lees, and several other top birders.' As a teaser Guy added 'You can even photograph Red Kites.' That did it. At that time Britain had only about a dozen pairs of Red Kites, all in secluded valleys in Wales, and no photographer, not even the incomparable Hosking, had been allowed to intrude upon their privacy with his camera.

Eric needed no more persuasion and a few weeks later we all took off for the Coto Doñana, an old hunting preserve in the south of Spain where Red Kites are fairly common. In those days the Coto, with its Palacio, was almost exactly as it had been in the time of King Philip III, except for a few plantations of eucalyptus trees. The only modern note was a tractor which we sometimes used instead of horses for hauling our gear. James Fisher, impressed by the ancient cork oaks, the numerous wild boars, and the herds of red deer and fallow deer (we counted 108 in one mob), said that the Coto gave him an inkling of what wild England must have been like during the Middle Ages. He commented later, 'I half expected King Henry the Eighth to ride by.'

A few days later Eric and I took our leave and engaged a big black Mercedes and a chauffeur (the only conveyance we could get) and made the journey through the vast rolling grain fields north of Jerez to the ancient town of Arcos where, from a cliff-top balcony, we photographed immense Griffon Vultures – fifty or sixty of them – as they glided past. Scores of Lesser Kestrels, small falcons, shared the cliffs with the vultures. Both of these birds are on the British list as accidental wanderers and were legitimate quarry. However, Eric could not resist the opportunity to photograph a number of Spanish species that had never been recorded in Britain. It was after that liberating experience that he decided to become a world traveller. Why be limited to the 450 species on the British list when there are nearly 9000 species of birds in the world? Many of them had never been photographed.

Ever since that first Spanish adventure it has been difficult to keep Eric Hosking on home turf. He has since ranged across Europe from the Mediterranean to Scandinavia and from Britain eastward to Bulgaria and Hungary. He has explored the deserts of Jordan and Tunisia as well as the more humid terrain of the Indian subcontinent. He has sailed in the wake of Darwin to the Galapagos where long lenses are not needed and has gone on safari in East Africa.

Eric Hosking has been called the world's greatest bird photographer and I believe this is an accurate assessment. In North America there have been giants, too: men such as Dr Arthur A. Allen, America's first professor of ornithology, who pioneered some of the techniques that later became standard; the late Allan Cruickshank, who perhaps came closest to being like Eric Hosking in his fine black and white portraiture of

North American species; and Elliott Porter, a great technician, who has brought his colour portraiture of birds to a high degree of artistry. Eric Hosking embodies the virtues of all three. When one considers the volume of his work and its long history, progressing from a Box Brownie to the most sophisticated of present-day equipment, he has no peer, although he would disagree, generously pointing to others whom he admires.

It is an education for any photographer, or for any birdwatcher for that matter, to be in the field with Eric Hosking. His intimacy with some birds, I daresay, cannot be matched. Long hours in the hide have given him insights into the behaviour of many species that escape the watcher with the binoculars.

Eric has a great eye for a picture and one eye is all he seems to need. As everyone knows, he lost the other to a Tawny Owl in a photographic mishap. But this did not stop him from photographing owls.

Photography, like painting, is primarily seeing. The main difference is that a photograph is the record of a moment, a split second, whereas a painting is (or should be) a composite of the artist's experience. The artist contrives, improvises, edits out. But whereas the mind perceives a subject in a certain way, the camera, a very impersonal instrument, does not. To make the camera behave, and to emphasize precisely what was in the eye of the beholder, requires great skill in manipulating photographic angles, lenses of various focal lengths, exposures, filters and darkroom work. And then there is the element of chance. As Eric Hosking points out in his autobiography *An Eye for a Bird* (Hutchinson, 1970), one or two photographs of a series always stand out above the rest. There is just one fleeting moment when everything is right. Once when working with Barn Owls he made 365 exposures to get the one that stood out above all the others, his most famous photograph – the Barn Owl in a heraldic pose.

Eric Hosking should be honoured not only for his skill as a photographer, but also for what he has done to build on the tradition of birdwatching initiated by Gilbert White more than two centuries ago. Had it not been for the birdwatchers we might not have seen the environmental movement as we know it today. Birds, because of their high rate of metabolism and their furious pace of living, are sensitive indicators of the environment – a sort of ecological litmus paper. They are an early warning system, sending out signals when there are changes in the countryside, changes that might ultimately affect man as well. It is therefore no accident that most of the officers of the leading conservation organizations in the world either are birdwatchers or were birdwatchers. Photographers such as Eric Hosking, the wildlife artists, and the nature writers have played a major role in creating the climate – the public awareness – that sparked the environmental movement.

Roger Tory Peterson

Fifty Years of Bird Photography

Natural history captured my imagination some six years before I became interested in photography, for while at two or three I was collecting insects in matchboxes it was not until the age of eight that my parents gave me a five-shilling Box Brownie (how many professional photographers have started their career with that same make of camera?). The results were not exactly outstanding but by literally saving up my pennies for the next two years I was eventually able to buy a magnificent 1909 Sanderson Field Camera with a mahogany body and brass fittings that took 4¼″ x 3¼″ plates; it came from a stall in the old Farringdon Market in London, now, alas, a pale shadow of its former amazing self, but where in those days you could buy anything from first editions to cabbages. The camera had a focusing screen but no lens or darkslides. After much haggling I paid thirty shillings for this camera, which I used for all my serious natural history work until 1947.

A lens and some darkslides came next. Once the camera had been put together my father bought me a dozen plates, the darkslides were loaded and off I rushed to a Song Thrush's nest to take my very first natural history photograph. It was a disaster. I had not realized there was anything more to photography than pointing the camera in the right direction and pressing the shutter release; focusing was outside my technical knowledge.

However, I rapidly gained experience and joined both the photographic and natural history societies at school, where much of my spare time was spent looking for nests and listening to owls in the woods at dusk instead of doing homework. My boyhood heroes were the famous Kearton brothers, and when Richard came to lecture to the school and I was allowed to meet him at the station and carry his slides I was near to heaven.

At that time it took little more than five minutes to cycle from the North London suburb in which we lived out into the fields and hedgerows that had hardly changed for a century. In some ways it was the best of both worlds, living so close to London yet with unspoilt country almost on our doorstep; today it takes half an hour's driving before you are free of the houses.

Leaving school at fifteen for a dull office job, I thought at the time it was teaching me very little, but I acquired the rudiments of methodical filing and record-keeping, a good foundation for professional photography. Then the Great Depression of 1929 brought unemployment and misery until I was asked to take a picture of a young sea elephant at the Zoo, for which I was paid the then huge sum of two guineas. The die was cast and I decided

The 1909 Sanderson Field Camera within the framework of a typical hide. The Luc shutter is fitted behind the lens, and the long antinus release hangs down conveniently for me to fire the shutter from the seated position.

A Long-tailed Tit at its nest with the young begging for food: one of my very early photographs, taken with the Sanderson Field Camera in 1930.

13

The Sanderson Field Camera used in conjunction with a Soho Reflex to take photographs of the Montagu's Harrier. The female flying down to the nest was taken with one camera, focused just above the nest. The other camera, focused on the nest, recorded the brief visit of the cock, to the right in the picture above.

to become the first full-time photographer of natural history, fifty years ago.

Since then I have only worked for myself and have never regretted it, though the life of a freelance photographer involves impossible hours, few holidays and extraordinary variations in income. It is especially hard on wives and I am indeed fortunate to be married to Dorothy, who shares my work, worries and interests.

A major problem when taking photographs in those days was that the emulsions then available were by modern standards very slow and if you stopped down the lens sufficiently to get the whole of a nest sharp the exposure became very long. The Sanderson, however, had every imaginable movement and the back could be tilted to obtain great depth of field even though a comparatively large stop was being used. The disadvantage was, of course, that it took time to change the plate and recock the shutter every time you took a picture, and once the plates in my holders were used up I had to go into a dark-room or use a changing bag to reload.

I used a Luc shutter behind the lens, a very silent affair that gave short exposures if you pressed the cable release fast and long ones if you pressed it slowly, a real help in changing light. The slight click at the end of the exposure did not matter since it came after the picture had been taken, but the exposures were not accurate enough for colour work.

To start with I used Wellington Anti-Screen plates which were orthochromatic, that is they were insensitive to red light so that reddish objects appeared black in the photographs. This was a serious snag and I remember taking a picture of an Oystercatcher in which you could not distinguish the red eye from the head since they came out in the same tone. Then panchromatic plates, which were equally sensitive to all colours, came on the market and for many years I used Ilford Soft Gradation Pan for work in good light and Hypersensitive Pan in dull weather.

Of course I developed all my own negatives and liked to experiment with different developers and different techniques to get exactly the right gradation. Standardization has taken a lot of the craftsmanship out of photography; who now adds a little more metol, hydroquinone or bromide to a formula to alter the contrast or speed? It became a firm rule at the end of the day's field work to develop my plates in a Dallon Daylight Developing Tank so that the results could be seen at once and consequently the photographs repeated if anything had gone wrong. These days you send your colour films away to be processed and by the time they come back the young have left the nest.

It really was very important to keep a check on what was happening if you were far away from base. I remember a friend of mine, a superb natural history photographer, going up to the Shetlands by boat (no planes in those days) and in an effort to save weight leaving all his processing equipment at home. After a

month's wonderful photography he returned and developed his plates to find that every one of them was fogged. There was a moth lava that loved leather bellows and it had nibbled a tiny hole in one corner, invisible when he looked at the focusing screen but large enough for light to enter and build up while he waited patiently for a bird to arrive.

My first real field work was done in East Anglia in 1930, living almost entirely on rabbits with a gamekeeper and his daughter in Suffolk. I soon found that though birds were my main interest, it would be essential to build up a library of all kinds of nature pictures if I were to survive as the only professional natural history photographer in the business. I therefore took pictures of anything that might sell – insects, mammals or plants. In 1934 a Model 1 Leica was added to my equipment, a basic 35mm camera that was used with a separate, uncoupled rangefinder. It served me until 1947 when it was replaced by a Contax which had a bigger range of lenses and, most important, a bayonet mount which made changing lenses in a hide much quicker and easier than with the screw mount of the Leica.

After experimenting with Dufaycolour Film, which needed a lot of exposure and had a criss-cross pattern of coloured lines over it which prevented much in the way of enlargement, my first serious colour pictures were taken in 1935 using the Leica and the new Kodachrome film. It was slow, 10 ASA, and the colours were not very accurate. In the same year I used the first Sashalite flashbulbs, which revolutionized nature photography. Up till then I had tried to take pictures at night with flash powder, not very successfully. The trouble was that the flash, a minor explosion, took about a second to complete. It is amazing how far a bird can travel in that time – the result was usually just a blur.

It was Lord Alanbrooke, working out in India, who devised one of the first methods of synchronizing the flash with the shutter. He put the powder in a metal box with a hinged lid, connected to the shutter via a cable release; as the flash went off the lid was knocked violently upwards and the shutter, set perhaps at 1/50th of a second, was released. The snag was that emulsions were so slow you had to use a great deal of powder, and once when working from a hide he set fire to a whole tree which had to be put out by the local fire brigade. In those days nature photography was never dull.

So when GEC marketed the first Sashalites and gave me ten to test, the first ever used for natural history work in Britain, I went up to Suffolk and tried them out on a Barn Owl, finding them absolutely invaluable. About the size of a modern 100 watt bulb, they were filled with crumpled aluminium foil in oxygen and gave a flash that lasted for about 1/30th of a second, too long for any bird

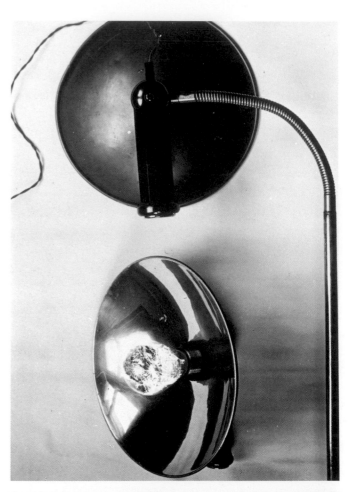

A Barn Owl hide with Sashalite flashlight equipment attached at an upper corner, and a close-up view of the equipment from front and rear. After each exposure it was necessary to reach out through a hole in the hide and change the bulb. The rear view of the reflector shows the flexible arm used for adjusting the position and the wire which led to a press-button switch within the hide.

A Barn Owl brings a young rat to the nest. It was not until the negative was developed that I saw the rat was there. The Sashalite bulb fired at about 1/30th of a second, insufficient to stop the movement of the rat's tail.

that was moving. So the technique was to set up the camera and then, when it became totally dark, open the shutter and listen for the faint sound of the bird's claws as it landed on the branch. Then I would chirrup to make it look round, and immediately fire the bulb. It was surprising how often you heard imaginary birds landing. The bird of course flew off and then one had to reach up out of the hide to change the bulb, and then change the darkslide, before another picture could be taken.

In 1946 Dawe Instruments brought out one of the first 'portable' electronic flash units giving an exposure of 1/5000th of a second. This would stop all but the fastest movement of a bird, but the difficulty was that the current flowed all the time the unit was switched on and in ten minutes the battery was flat. Then an electronics expert named Dr Philip Henry came to my aid and added a device that switched off the battery when the condenser was fully charged and then on again as the charge fell. This helped a great deal but the light output was very low; it was not possible to use a stop small enough to get both wings of a flying bird in focus at the same time. So Dr Henry built me a fabulous affair that weighed over a hundredweight, running off a 24 volt battery that added another forty pounds to the weight. It was extremely successful, having an output of 670 watt-seconds with the short duration of 1/5000th of a second (most modern high-capacity units have a duration of about 1/700th, which is far too long), but it took an awful lot of energy to transport it to a remote location.

The next problem to be solved was that a bird four feet in front of the camera flying at only 25 miles per hour was in the field of view for just 1/10th of a second, and the photographer's reactions are not fast enough to press the release at the right moment. So Dr Henry devised a system whereby the birds photographed themselves by cutting a beam of light thrown on to a photo-electric cell, and some of our troubles were over.

My first 35mm single lens reflex was the Exakta. Though I appreciated the ease with which telephoto lenses could be focused and the way in which I could see exactly what was being included in the picture, it was by no means an ideal camera since the image was reversed left to right in the viewfinder, making it very difficult to follow moving objects, and it was hard to take vertical pictures. In 1963 Zeiss Ikon introduced the Contarex, a 35mm reflex fitted with a pentaprism which gave a right way up and right way round image in the finder, whether the camera was held horizontally or vertically. It had a wonderful selection of superb lenses, and magazine backs that allowed me to change from colour to black and white at will. I used the various models for a long time, all

beautiful examples of German precision manufacture, the only real drawback being their weight.

Both Dorothy and I found this to be a real disadvantage, particularly in the tropics, and one day in Africa an American doctor showed us one of the first Olympus OM-1s, light, compact and precise. Dorothy, who does all the background photography of scenery, people, etc. while I photograph wild life, said 'I'd be happy using that' and since Zeiss Ikon ceased camera production about the same time I changed to the Olympus OM-1s and then, as soon as they came on the market, to the fully automatic OM-2s. I have had five of them, which have been used to take tens of thousands of pictures in many parts of the world, the only breakdown being caused by a speck of grit on one of the synchronizing contacts.

I also use the 6cm x 6cm Hasselblad, partly because of the superb quality of the results but also because many publishers still cannot be bothered to examine the small 35mm transparencies properly. Using Kodachrome 64 the Olympus camera can give results

Wooden pylon hide erected in the Coto Doñana in southern Spain for photographing Short-toed Eagles (see pages 60-1). Note the pole linking the tree to the hide which kept the nest in focus as the tree swayed.

A hide erected on the Little Eye, Hilbre. As the tide rises the Oystercatchers are already gathering at the tip of the rocky tongue *(arrowed)* on which the hide stands, and they will gradually be driven towards it. A typical photograph taken from this kind of hide shows Oystercatcher, Redshank and Knot.

A semi-permanent 'wait and see' hide erected by a stream. Two high-speed flash lamps are directed onto a rock placed in the water as a convenient perch *(arrowed)*. A cock House Sparrow perches on the rock after bathing *(above)*.

A hide erected on the steep slope of a cliff by the nest *(arrowed)* of a pair of Buzzards. The hide is anchored in position by ropes. In a photograph taken from this hide the two young are sound asleep after being fed by the adult on a rabbit.

that will enlarge up to almost any size, but the 6cm x 6cm transparencies are more eye-catching. However, the beautifully made Hasselblad equipment, in particular the long focus lenses, can become very heavy indeed if you are climbing hills and mountains, and it is possible, having arrived at the location, to be almost too exhausted to take pictures. Both the Olympus OM-1 and the Hasselblad have mirrors that, after the picture has been focused and composed, can be raised without releasing the shutter, thus reducing camera noise when the moment actually comes to take the picture. This is an asset when working from a hide, from which so many of my pictures are taken. Hides of several different kinds that have served me over the years are illustrated here.

All my pictures are now taken on colour film, Kodachrome and Ektachrome 64 in normal light and Ektachrome 200 and 400 when the action is rapid. I find the OM-2 with its fully automatic exposure setting a great advantage, especially in Britain with its rapidly changing light. In Africa, for instance, where the light remains constant you can set the controls on a camera and take picture after picture without having to alter them, but when working from a hide in Britain it is difficult to have to keep changing the stop or shutter speed as clouds pass across the sun.

Automation is a good thing provided you have a sound basic knowledge of the principles of photography so that you know what is going on. The Olympus Auto-Quick 310 automatic electronic flash, for example, has been most useful. I much appreciated it when photographing the Seychelles Bare-legged Scops Owl (see page 173) that kept flying from branch to branch, one moment four feet from the camera and the next ten. In the old days of manual setting it would have been difficult to calculate what stop you should be using at any given moment, but the automatic flash gave the correct exposure – all I had to do was to focus and frame the subject.

These days I am doing a lot of work with my son David on the development of a new portable high-speed flash outfit that has replaced the very efficient but very heavy one designed by Philip Henry so long ago. The old apparatus developed a fault that could not be rectified and years later when talking on Hilbre Island to Professor J.D. Craggs, Head of the Department of Electrical Engineering and Electronics at Liverpool University, I mentioned how much David and I wanted to get back to taking flight photographs of our smaller birds. The photo cell units commercially available could not be used since there was too great a delay between the beam of light being cut and the camera shutter being released – birds move very fast

when flying – while the electronic flashes either had too long a duration or did not have enough power. To stop the movement of a bird's wings a flash duration at least as short as 1/10,000th of a second is needed and the flash has to be bright enough to let us use a stop of f16 with colour film, preferably 64 ASA in speed.

Professor Craggs soon introduced us to an electronic wizard named Paul Watkinson who adapted two Braun 280 computerized 'automatic' flash units to give a constant flash duration of 1/10,000th and linked them together through a control box. This stopped all movement very successfully, but the light output was insufficient to let us use a small enough aperture even with 200 ASA film; we could not get enough depth of field to get the whole of a bird into focus. So he added another six Braun units to make two banks of four flash heads each, and this largely solved our problems. Even when using 64 ASA film we can use a stop small enough to make the whole bird sharp – provided it is in exactly the right place when the flash is fired.

We use the Hasselblad with a 150 or 250mm lens for much of this flight photography and we realized right from the start that if it was operated in the normal fashion there would be too great a delay between the solenoid operating the shutter release and the picture being taken. A lot of mechanical things happen inside the Hasselblad before the Compur shutter is released and, while it all takes place in a fraction of a second and in normal conditions seems almost instantaneous, a fast-moving bird would have long gone by the time the picture was actually taken.

In order to obtain a minimum of delay between the breaking of the beam by the bird and the firing of the shutter we still use the very rapid and powerful solenoid designed by Philip Henry – no one has found anything better. To avoid the slight delay that takes place in the firing of the Hasselblad shutter we placed a very old but very rugged Ilex shutter in front of the lens and fitted the solenoid release to it instead. The sequence now is to focus the Hasselblad with the Ilex shutter open, close it, set the camera as though we were making a time exposure and then take the picture with the Ilex. It sounds a rather roundabout way of working but it gives us the results.

Much work remains to be done and we would like to obtain still more power without lengthening the flash duration. We are also experimenting with two systems of rapid-sequence photography. In the first we use an Olympus fitted with a 5 frames per second motor drive and an adjustment to the control box that will fire the flash units in sequence as exposures are made. For the second we use the Hasselblad, firing several flash units with a very brief delay between

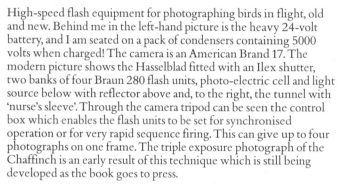

High-speed flash equipment for photographing birds in flight, old and new. Behind me in the left-hand picture is the heavy 24-volt battery, and I am seated on a pack of condensers containing 5000 volts when charged! The camera is an American Brand 17. The modern picture shows the Hasselblad fitted with an Ilex shutter, two banks of four Braun 280 flash units, photo-electric cell and light source below with reflector above and, to the right, the tunnel with 'nurse's sleeve'. Through the camera tripod can be seen the control box which enables the flash units to be set for synchronised operation or for very rapid sequence firing. This can give up to four photographs on one frame. The triple exposure photograph of the Chaffinch is an early result of this technique which is still being developed as the book goes to press.

them during the period that the camera shutter remains open. This gives a sequence of pictures of the bird and its wing movements on a single frame of film and our first results have been very exciting indeed.

Much experience has been gained since I worked with the flash unit built for me by Dr Henry and we can now work in locations that we could never have reached if in addition to our cameras we had to carry 150 pounds of flash equipment. It is hard to say what future electronic developments are in store but the photography of birds in flight becomes more and more exciting as time goes by.

The next thing to come will probably be automatic focusing, which will be useful for action work provided you can switch it off and focus visually when necessary. Films and lenses will become sharper and faster, lighter and more powerful flash units will appear and photographic equipment will generally become more portable. Then will come video tape and we shall have to relearn our technique!

Good natural history photography will always, however, be largely a matter of knowledge, experience and patience. Until people are better educated in the preservation of wildlife there will still be photo-

graphers who are only interested in the final picture and do not care how they get it. I am sorry to say I have seen tired, hungry and disorientated birds, who only want to rest and eat in peace, being driven from one side of a marsh to another by batteries of amateur cameramen and birdwatchers. A true bird photographer, on the other hand, is primarily interested in the welfare of the birds and will go to great trouble to disturb them as little as possible, perhaps carefully tying back a twig that obscures his view of a nest with very fine black thread while he takes his picture and then carefully replacing the foliage and leaving everything exactly as he found it. *The birds must come first.*

Looking back at my career, I often think how fortunate it is that I can earn my living by following such an absorbing hobby. My son David, equally interested, is carrying on the work with very advanced equipment and is producing superb results. However, though in another fifty years his present equipment will probably seem as dated as the Sanderson Field Camera with which I started, and which I still possess, I am sure the fascination of bird photography will still be as great as it was in those pioneering days fifty years ago.

The Fascination of Birds

Preceding page The Nightingale, a wonderful songster best heard during the hours of darkness.

Opposite A cock Nightjar hovering above its nest. The primaries of the farther wing are bent right forward. The large eye is typical of a nocturnal bird.

Above The first time I ever photographed the Greenshank's shell disposal. Sir Julian Huxley called this my best picture.

Whether we realize it or not, deep within most of us is a desire to create. For some people it takes the form of drawing or painting, for others it lies in music. Some compete in the field of sport, others seek this satisfaction in the open countryside. Nearly all my life I have been utterly devoted to animals, especially to birds, and most of my waking hours have been spent watching, studying and photographing them. The attraction of birds for me lies in observing their natural behaviour without being seen. London has been my home for almost all my life and I have no wish to live anywhere else, but such is the appeal of the birds that whenever the skies are blue and the sun shines I feel compelled to take up my camera and get away into the countryside.

The feeling is greatest in the spring when the days lengthen, the new green foliage bursts forth and the wild birds start their chorus. Before the first migrants return to British shores the Blackbird and the Song Thrush are already in full song and the Mistle Thrush is singing wildly from the tops of the trees. Then, almost as soon as the visitors arrive they, too, commence singing, not for our benefit but to proclaim a territory in which they can breed. The beauty of the song of the Nightingale can bring tears to my eyes and it is hard to believe that it is really a battle cry, a warning to all other Nightingales that the ground from which he sings is his property and that intruders will be repelled. There will be only one exception – the female he is trying to court.

While some birds have lovely songs, others fascinate me with their colourful plumage. Within five minutes' drive of our home there are local reservoirs which have a resident pair of Kingfishers. In the spring, if I sit

Above The hen Snowy Owl glares at the camera lens after alighting at her nest. This was the first recorded nesting in the British Isles of this magnificent bird of the Arctic wastes.

Opposite A cock Marsh Harrier alighting at the nest, one of the rarest British breeding birds.

quietly with my back against the trunk of a tree, they often come within a few yards of me. Their gorgeous, iridescent chestnut and blue plumage almost takes my breath away by its sheer loveliness. As I watch, the cock suddenly dives into the water, emerges a moment later with a small fish in his bill and returns to his perch. As he does so the hen quivers her wings and begs to be fed, just like a baby bird in the nest. Before making the offering to her he bangs it several times against the branch to kill it. As she takes the fish from him he leaps in the air, hovers for a moment, alights on her back and they mate.

One of my greatest challenges has been to try to photograph birds in flight. To stand near the edge of a sea cliff and attempt to get shots of the gulls as they glide by on the updraft is indeed exhilarating, but the thrill is even greater when in the Galapagos Islands that great rarity the Waved Albatross sweeps by, often no more than twenty feet away.

To portray the small birds in flight is almost impossible without some technical aid, and it has given my son David and me a great thrill to use some of the latest developments in electronics to achieve the results we want. Because the human eye, brain and

Opposite The Tawny Owl that robbed me of an eye, squeezing into its nest. I do not blame it for attacking me but rather admire the way in which it sought to defend its young.

Above One of my earliest successes. This photograph of Britain's royal bird later became universally familiar as the trademark of Swan Vestas matches.

fingers are so slow we have to let the bird take its own picture by using a photo-electric shutter release.

Birds of prey, both diurnal and nocturnal, have always had a special place in my life. Dorothy, my wife, always claims that though we were married forty years ago we have still not been on honeymoon, for we spent three months after the ceremony in the Scottish Highlands searching for and photographing the magnificent Golden Eagle at its eyrie. Perhaps she is right because we visited some pretty remote places, climbed some almost sheer mountains and by night

time were quite exhausted! Because of the difficulty of getting to and from the hide, perched on a cliff face with a drop of three hundred feet below, I used to spend forty-eight hours in it at a stretch. What a thrill it was to see the King of the Birds at such close quarters. I often felt that its piercing gaze was going right through the hide, watching me just as closely as I was watching it.

However, there can be no doubt that my favourites in the whole world of birds are the owls, those amazing birds of the night. I have spent many hours

A Masked Booby in soaring flight, photographed in the Galapagos Islands, epitomizes effortless mastery of the air.

alone in utter darkness listening for the owl to return to its nest and hoping I would hear its talons touch down. The owls are silent fliers and when using the automatic photo-electric shutter release I have often almost jumped out of my skin when the flash has suddenly and unexpectedly gone off as the ghostly figure interrupted the circuit.

If anyone asked me what it is that so fascinates me about birds, why I become so completely absorbed when photographing them, I would not be able to give a direct answer. Indeed, I would probably reply by asking a question myself – what is it that makes a golfer want to hit a small, white ball on smooth, green turf; what makes a fisherman sit on the bank of a river for hour after hour watching a tiny float, waiting for it to start bobbing; what makes the mountaineer pit his puny strength against the great mountains of the world? One ball holed, one fish caught, one peak conquered or, for me, one successful bird photograph makes all the waiting, the risk, the planning and scheming worthwhile.

Birds of the Night

Overleaf and above A Little Owl in flight and another standing at the entrance to its nesting hole. Each has an earthworm in its bill. Pictures like these helped to prove that the Little Owl is not a predator of game chicks, but feeds mainly on invertebrates.

Opposite Snowy Owls. The almost pure white cock *(above)* pays a brief visit to the nest with an immature Oystercatcher he has caught. The streaked and spotted female alights at the nest *(below)*. This picture was reproduced across a whole page in *The Times*.

For as long as I can remember, owls have completely fascinated me. As a boy I often used to be missing from home at bedtime but my parents did not worry because they knew just where to find me – in our local playing fields watching and listening to Tawny Owls. There was not a tree in the fields I had not climbed and I knew the nest of every Tawny in the neighbourhood. Their hooting made my blood tingle and nothing absorbed me more than hearing two cocks hooting and calling against each other.

When a Tawny reaches maturity it has to find a territory of its own and the only way it can do this is to fly from one wood to another, or if the wood is very large to various parts of it. The owl stops and calls and if not challenged it may go deeper into the wood and call again. Sooner or later it will be heard by another Tawny, be challenged and retreat. In this way, by trial and error, it finally establishes a safe territory of its own.

The owl hoots not only to establish his territory but to attract a female so that they can nest together. The

Above A Short-eared Owl adopts an aggressive pose while brooding over her young.

Opposite The development of an aggressive display in an African Barn Owl. In the last picture the bird's attention is being diverted from below.

hen has a different call and when they meet, instead of adopting an aggressive pose as would another male, she appears submissive. Together they inspect various holes in trees, rabbit holes or perhaps the abandoned nests of Carrion Crows, Magpies or Sparrow Hawks, but if none of these appeals to the female they may even decide to nest on the ground.

The breeding behaviour of most British owls is similar, none of them building their own nest but just laying their eggs on the bare surface of the place they have chosen. Incubation, by the hen only, usually starts after the first egg has been laid, though there are ex-

ceptions. The intervals between the laying of the eggs varies according to the species; in the case of the Little Owl, for instance, an egg is usually laid each day but with the Barn Owl there can be an interval of several days in between. This means of course that the young hatch at intervals and because some owls lay as many as eight or more eggs the first one to be hatched can be quite large by the time the youngest is born.

When you approach the nest of some owls, the parents may well resent your presence and attack you. During the last fifty years I have been actually hit by three of them – Tawny, Little and Short-eared Owls.

Above and opposite A series of photographs showing the different wing positions as a Barn Owl returns to its nest inside a Suffolk barn. Several visits were recorded as the owl flew up from the broken window at which it alighted on entering the barn. There are several fascinating instances of the flexions of the wings as the bird gains height.

The first mentioned attacked me in the pitch darkness of the night as I climbed the pylon hide that had been erected near its nest, flying like all owls absolutely silently, and I had no idea it was anywhere near until it struck the left side of my face, its claw penetrating right into my eye. Cyril Newberry, co-author with me of several books, was present at the time, and he at once drove me all the way from Central Wales to the Moorfields Eye Hospital in London. Back in 1937 there were no modern antibiotics and when the disease of ophthalmia set in there was a great risk that through sympathetic action it would spread across to the right eye.

It was a real dilemma – risk keeping both eyes and going completely blind or have the injured eye removed. There were twenty-four hours in which to make the decision. I thought of those fine bird photographers and ornithologists Walter Higham and Geoffrey Ingram who both had only one eye; after all only one eye is used when taking photographs. So the

operation was performed but it is sad to think that had the accident occurred today it is almost certain that both the eye and its sight would have been saved by the use of modern drugs. One thing must be made quite clear – I attach no blame whatever to the owl who thought her young were threatened and was prepared to defend them.

Just as the hoot of a Tawny Owl excites me, so the eerie screech of the Barn Owl makes my blood run cold. It is always so sudden and unexpected: it is easy to understand how people walking through a cemetery after dark, seeing a pure white apparition swooping towards them from a tree or a tombstone, hovering above their head and then uttering a shriek, are sure they have both seen and heard a ghost.

In 1948 the nest of a Barn Owl was found in a corn-hopper in an old Suffolk barn, the only entrance for the owls being through a broken window. By setting up a photo-electric shutter release I was able to let the owls take their own photographs as they flew up from the

Above Immature Spotted Eagle Owl photographed in Rhodesia.

Opposite This lovely cock Snowy Owl, born in captivity at Chester Zoo, has to go through one more moult before achieving the pure white plumage of the adult male.

window towards their nest, using a flash exposure of 1/5000th of a second. Throughout many all-night watches, 365 exposures were made. One of the pictures stood out above all the others and has become my most famous photograph – the Barn Owl in a heraldic pose (pages 42-3).

Also in Suffolk, in the following year, 1949, we found a pair of Little Owls nesting in a hole in a tree only about five feet above ground and once again using the automatic shutter release with the high-speed flash many photographs were taken. The results showed a great variety of food being brought to the young –

worms, ants, beetles, moths and a field mouse.

Unfortunately, we did not have the high-speed flash equipment in 1940 when photographing the Long-eared Owl in Norfolk and had to use the old Sashalite bulbs (see the first chapter). After each picture the bulb had to be changed and great care was needed not to disturb the adults. Life was not made any easier for us by the fact that the Long-eared Owl is the most nocturnal of all the British owls. Unless it is disturbed from its nesting or roosting place it is rarely seen about in daylight. It may, of course, hunt for food during the day following a night of rain, or in mid-winter when

Opposite The Great Horned Owl, the largest owl of the North American continent.

The Eagle Owl, Europe's largest owl, at its nest under a rock face in Norway *(above)* and giving a full threat display *(overleaf)* in response to the approach of the camera. The colour photograph was taken from not more than three feet away in a private aviary.

the rodents which are its normal diet tend to sleep in a warm place through some of the bitter cold nights.

The flash duration of the bulb was about 1/30th of a second, a comparatively long time. Many exposures were spoilt because of movement and one that might have been a winner was of the cock giving the hen a young rat. We noticed an interesting sidelight in that the cock knew exactly when the young were hatching. Up till this moment he had not left any food at the nest but with the hatching of the first tiny chick, covered in soft, white

down and with its eyes not yet open, food was left with the hen. Was the hen able to communicate in some way to the cock that the hatching had started?

We were fascinated by the way in which the Long-eared Owls were able to fly through the densely inter-twining twigs of the pine trees without colliding with them and could come unerringly to the nest on even the darkest night. Owls have wonderfully sensitive eyes which can take full advantage of even the smallest amount of light, though if there is no light whatever they

My most famous photograph, the Barn Owl caught in heraldic pose as it flies into a barn in Suffolk with a vole gripped in its bill; the culminating picture of the series shown on pages 34-5.

cannot see. The eyes are so large that they occupy most of the skull and, as Dr Stuart Smith explained in his chapter in the book I wrote with Cyril Newberry, *Birds of the Night* (Collins, 1948), they are so tightly jammed into the sockets that they cannot be moved. This, however, is compensated for superbly by the extraordinary way in which the owls can swivel their heads round through three-quarters of a circle so that they can see over their backs.

Another wonderful thing about them is the nictitating eyelid, which all birds possess but which in the case of the owl is opaque, whereas with most birds it is transparent. It is used to wash the huge eyes and keep them free from dust and dirt, while its outer surface cleans the inside of the eyelid. Incidentally, we humans used to have a third

Two typical zoo studies taken in the portable studio showing a Little Owl *(opposite)* and a Screech Owl *(above).*

or nictitating eyelid but it became atrophied through lack of use, though a trace of it can still be seen in the nasal corners of our eyes, a little crescent-shaped button.

If the Long-eared is the most nocturnal of our owls the Short-eared is the most diurnal and can often be seen flying over marsh, heather and moor during the day. However, it does not usually feed its young during the day, preferring a concentrated period in the evening and around dawn. At the nests I have watched, voles have been by far their favourite food and the supply seems to determine the breeding distribution of the Short-eared Owl in Britain. During the vole plague years, for inst-

ance, Short-eared Owls become quite common in the areas where these rodents are found. They then lay large clutches of eggs, increasing the number from the normal four or five to thirteen or even fourteen and they usually succeed in rearing these large families. At such times the voles can be seen piled high up around the nest, the number being far in excess of the amount the young owls can possibly consume.

The gorgeous Snowy Owl is a bird that is usually associated with the icy wastes of the arctic regions. In 1967 that fine Shetland ornithologist and RSPB warden Bobby Tulloch discovered a pair nesting and I was invited

Above Long-eared Owl perched above its nest, containing eggs. The 'ear tufts', which have nothing to do with the actual ears, are erected.

Opposite A Long-eared Owl bringing an immature rat to the nest, on which the female is brooding over the newly-hatched young. Here the ear tufts are lowered.

to try to obtain photographs of the first-ever recorded breeding in the British Isles.

Dorothy and I flew to Sumburgh in the Shetlands and then by bus and boat we made our way to Mid Yell where Bobby met us. Next day he took us over to Fetlar and to a point where the nest could be seen through binoculars. For a while the white body of the bird was invisible against rocky outcrops, but after careful directions I spotted it. Within a couple of hours of arriving on Fetlar I was sitting on my own in the hide which Dennis Coutts of Lerwick had erected in advance. A few minutes later

the hen Snowy alighted a few yards away, waddled to the nest and settled down to brood.

Then happened an incident that almost doubled me up with laughter though I knew no sound must be made. The owl caught the reflection of her face in the camera lens and started to tilt her head sideways more and more until finally her face was completely upside down. But she was carefully noting everything that was going on and she would have spotted the mirror flying up as she looked through the lens if I had taken a photograph. Until she got used to it this movement could frighten her

An African Marsh Owl photographed at night in Rhodesia collecting bait.

away. It was a moment of immense responsibility for if she deserted the nest not only would my name be mud but I would discredit all bird photographers. So waiting until she had settled down and was occupied in tucking the young under her, I made the first exposure and was happy to see that she did not seem to notice the slight noise made by the shutter and the mirror movement. Many wonderful hours were spent inside that hide over a period of days and a long series of pictures resulted, some of which were reproduced in *The Times* and other newspapers and magazines, as well as being shown on television.

The Snowy Owls have bred again several times but unfortunately the cock is now missing, so for the last year or two no eggs have been laid. I wonder if it would be possible to introduce another male.

So far we have photographed 41 of the 130 species of owls throughout the world, so there is still a lot of work waiting to be done. They are my favourite birds and I hope to continue to photograph them for many years to come.

Feeding Young

Preceding page This Grasshopper Warbler has lost its balance while feeding its young and spreads its wings to steady itself.

Opposite The hungriest young Blackbird stretches up highest and gets the food.

Above Hungry Jays clamour to receive a share from the adult.

Some of the most fascinating moments in the life of a bird photographer are spent sitting in a hide watching the ways in which birds feed and care for their young. The great variety of methods they use is a constant source of interest to me.

Birds can be divided into two main groups. The 'nidifugous' have young that are open-eyed when hatched, covered with down and able to leave the nest all together usually within the first day, all the eggs hatching within a few hours at the most. The second group, the 'nidicolous', have young that are blind and quite helpless when they hatch and have to stay in the nest for a long period varying from, say, eight or nine days in the case of the Sky Lark to several months in the case of the albatrosses.

Watching Blackbirds at the nest I have often observed the way in which the food is shared out amongst the chicks. As the parent alights on the edge of the nest the young stretch up their heads and beg, but the hungriest chick of all begs more vigorously and

Opposite As with the Blackbird, the Song Thrush gives the food it has brought to the chick that begs most vigorously.

Some of the chicks were asleep when this Veery returned to the nest, so there was less competition for the meal.

After being away for some time the hen Linnet returns with enough seeds in her crop to feed all her hungry young.

manages to reach up just a little higher than any of the others, and all the food is pushed into its mouth. Having been fed, it sinks to the bottom of the nest to sleep off its meal and though it manages to beg when the parent comes back the next time it does not receive any of the food: it is the second hungriest chick that is successful. So it goes on until all the chicks have been fed, by which time, of course, the first one is the hungriest again. The competition for food is fierce and if a chick is injured or weakened in any way it is unlikely to survive.

The Grasshopper Warbler, the Jay, the Song Thrush and the Veery whose photographs appear here all feed their chicks in turn in a similar way.

The Linnet and most other seed-eating birds adopt a different method of feeding their young. In this case the adults forage for seeds and soften them in their crops, this taking a little time to happen. Then when they return to the nest all the young beg together and all are fed at the same time with more or less the same amount of food regurgitated from the crop; there is enough for everyone. However, instead of returning to

Most herons, like the Squacco *(opposite, above)*, regurgitate food in response to stroking or tugging of their bill by the chicks. With the gulls (Great Black-backed Gull *opposite, below)* the chicks tap at a bright spot on the bill of the parent to produce the same effect.

Above Young Wood Pigeons push their bills into the mouth of the adult on either side. An up-and-down movement pumps the 'milk' directly from the crop into their throats.

the nest every few minutes as the Blackbirds do they are away from the nest for intervals of half an hour or more between the feeds. Perhaps because of this, court-ship feeding is particularly characteristic of the seed-eaters (see page 202).

Heron-like birds catch fish, frogs, eels and perhaps even young birds and retain them in their crops. Then when they return to the nest the young stimulate the parent to regurgitate by stroking or tugging at the adult's bill. The parent bird begins to retch and then deposits the food on the nest where the young all squabble to get a share. This often results in a tug-of-war since the food has not been broken into pieces.

Doves and pigeons feed on vegetable matter which is converted into a milk-like substance. When the adult arrives back at the nest the two young standing one at either side force their bills into and down the parent's throat. Then they all move up and down together in unison which enables the adult to pump the fluid directly into the mouths of the young. Because they receive a really adequate meal on each visit they are fed only two or three times a day.

Stone Curlews. The male on the left is pointing out a small beetle, while the female calls the other chick away from the nest.

A Merlin holds out a fragment of meat and calls softly to encourage its twelve-day-old chick to take it *(opposite, above)*. At the end of each meal these young Merlins were so satiated that they sprawled out flat in the bottom of the nest: photographs before *(centre)* and after.

Nidifugous birds fend for themselves from a very early stage. Soon after hatching (or if they do not hatch until evening, on the following day), when they are sufficiently dry and strong, the chicks are led from the nest and then the parent will point out with its bill a small beetle or spider, or a worm or some similar invertebrate, and the chick will run forward and grab it.

Once while at the nest of a Stone Curlew I was watching the hen brooding her two newly hatched young, one of which was still not dry. On the approach of the male, the elder chick came out from under the female and tottered across to the cock. He pointed out

a tiny beetle but every time the chick tried to catch it the beetle managed to wriggle free. So the cock bit the beetle to immobilize it and then dropped it in front of the youngster who quickly swallowed it. This is the kind of intimate scene that makes bird photography from a hide so fascinating.

I have happy memories of watching two young Buzzards covered in white down waiting to be fed. The mother was tenderness itself, ripping off a morsel of the rabbit which she gripped in her talons and holding it delicately in front of one of the nestlings. The youngster was so small that its eyes had not yet opened

and its head rolled around drunkenly trying to find the food; finally it touched it and opened its bill and the mother daintily put the food inside, at the same time cooing, coaxing and encouraging the nestling. With the utmost patience, when a fragment fell out of the chick's mouth she picked it up and started all over again.

Owls, who usually start incubation with the laying of the first egg and have young of varying ages, use a similar technique but brood over their young while they are still very small, passing food down to them. One of the reasons for this is that while the owl chicks are fed mainly at dusk they are sometimes also fed during the much colder period during the night and around dawn, when they need the warmth of the parent's body in order to survive. It must also be remembered that while many birds construct warm and comfortable nests, others make use of old, deserted

In a similar incident to that described below the cock Short-toed Eagle alights above the nest *(left)*. The end of a water snake projects from his bill. The female rises from brooding the chicks to greet him. She takes the snake from him *(above)* and offers it to the chick as he prepares to leave the nest *(opposite, above)*. A short time later the chick has nearly finished swallowing the snake *(opposite, below)*.

ones or even have no nest at all. Some owls lay their eggs on bare ground or in a hole in a tree and unless the young were covered by a parent they would very quickly become too cold to survive.

Not all birds feed their young as daintily as does the Buzzard. Watching the eyrie of a Short-toed Eagle in Spain I saw an extraordinary incident when the hen brought back to the nest a water snake that was four times the total length of the young eaglet. As the parent started to regurgitate it the chick grabbed the other end and started to swallow. But when swallowing a snake you have to do so head first, otherwise the scales will catch up in the throat. As the head of the snake finally slithered from the eagle's bill the chick ejected the tail and started afresh at the head end. Birds digest food quickly and the snake slowly but surely disappeared, but it took the eaglet thirty-seven minutes to complete its gigantic meal, at the end of which it lay exhausted. However, within three-and-a-half hours it was hungry again and quite ready for its next meal.

Overleaf A Bittern chick tugs at its parent's bill to stimulate regurgitation. The last chick has only just hatched and the empty eggshell has not yet been removed.

Birds in Flight

Preceding page Sanderling circle round looking for a place to land as the tide rises at Hilbre Island.

Opposite Massed flight of Knot near Hilbre Island. The cloud of birds suddenly packs together, sweeps down almost to ground level, and spreads out as it rises up again.

Above Contrasting with the Knot, the almost solitary Great White Egret rises from a jheel or marshland lake in Pakistan.

At some time or other we have all envied the birds their power of flight, which has made them the most biologically successful group of animals that has ever existed. Once wings and feathers evolved they provided an escape from predators, a means of travelling great distances and crossing impassable barriers, a way of migrating to favourable climates, the ability to catch flying insects and access to safe living and breeding quarters. Little wonder that birds as a class have survived so well, developing over 8500 different species in the process.

A cross-section through a bird's wing from front to back would show an outline not unlike that of the wing of an aircraft; the air moves across the upper surface faster than it does across the lower. The faster the speed of the air the lower the pressure, and the difference in pressure produces lift.

A great deal about the flapping flight of birds has yet to be learnt. Essentially, as the wings beat downwards and forwards the trailing edge bends upwards under

65

Opposite A Herring Gull with wings raised high as it lifts off from the surface of the sea

Above A Black-tailed Godwit at Minsmere leaps into the air to fly from one feeding place to another.

the air pressure from below and so the bird is driven forward, in an action not unlike that of a propeller. Since the wing feathers overlap like tiles on a roof, the stiff leading edge of one feather lying above the flexible trailing edge of the one in front, the feathers separate on the upward and backward stroke and allow the air to pass through.

Much more complicated things happen in the very rapid wing movements of slow flight which occurs with most birds at take-off and landing and in some aerial manoeuvres. Some of the research in this area over the last thirty years was triggered off by the

publication of my early high-speed flash photographs, which appeared in some cases to contradict what was known about bird flight at that time.

Soaring land birds seek out upward currents caused by the wind striking hills and mountains, and look for thermals caused by uneven heating of the air, which is hotter over cities and bare fields than it is over forests and water. Seabirds like gulls and Fulmars soar on currents of air deflected upwards by sea cliffs or in the turbulence that results when a seaward wind passes over a cliff edge. Some oceanic birds like the albatrosses cover distance by alternately soaring up into

An Arctic Tern hovers over the sea, on the lookout for a sand eel or similar small fish.

Dunlin fly up a few feet into the air as the waves of the advancing tide break against the red sandstone rock of Hilbre Island.

the prevailing wind and gliding down with it.

Birds have anticipated many of the devices fitted to modern aircraft. At the leading edge of the wing, for instance, is the alula, sometimes called the 'bastard wing', which spreads forward to form a slot so as to reduce turbulence at low speeds; Handley-Page invented it fifty years ago. Sometimes when I have been in the cockpit of an airliner looking at panel upon panel crammed with instruments, I have thought of the way a hummingbird hovers and birds navigate during migration. Man has indeed a long way to go

before he can rival the flight of the birds.

There are two ways of photographing birds in flight, by using the available daylight or using high-speed electronic flash. Generally speaking, the larger birds such as gulls, vultures, eagles and albatrosses are best taken in daylight while flash is reserved for the smaller ones such as the tits, thrushes, sparrows and finches.

To take a good photograph of any bird in flight is a difficult task. It would be hard to estimate the number of pictures I have taken of gulls, for instance, that have

Two photographs of an Osprey arriving at the nest, taken in Connecticut from a hide erected by Roger Tory Peterson. The magnificent wingspan can be fully appreciated as the bird comes in to land *(above)*. A moment later the wings flap forward and the tail is spread out in full braking action.

A White-backed Vulture soars over a carcass in Bangladesh. The large wing area and slotted wing tips which reduce turbulence are ideal for slow soaring flight.

ended up in the wastepaper basket. So many factors can affect the result. If you are standing near the nest of a Common Gull it may start off by flying towards you but then, just as it seems to be getting near enough, it will veer away. Alternatively, it may come and hover above your head or approach from a low angle, but usually at the critical moment it will suddenly change direction.

If it is flying towards you directly, the most difficult problem is to obtain a critically sharp picture because by the time the lens has been focused and the shutter released it will almost certainly have moved out of the plane of sharpness. I find the most successful technique is, first of all, to watch the bird and see how close it comes before turning away – probably between twenty and thirty feet depending on the species. The lens is then set at twenty-five feet and the image is watched on the screen. Just before it becomes critically sharp the shutter release is pressed and by the time this has been done and the shutter has fired the bird will be in exactly the right place – with a little luck, that is!

Another exciting method of flight photography is to stand near the edge of a sea cliff taking pictures of the birds as they soar or hang hovering in the wind. Here

A Masked Booby glides low over the sea *(above)*. By supreme mastery of available air currents it stays airborne with little effort.

The flapping flight of Crowned Cranes, photographed over the East African plains soon after dawn *(opposite)*, is much more strenuous by contrast.

Free as a bird: the graceful flight of the Common Gull *(above and right)*

Opposite The Great Skua or Bonxie swoops down with feet lowered to strike a trespasser near its nest.

Above The Grey Heron's flight is leisurely, with very slow wing beats. The neck is drawn in and the feet are held out behind to reduce air resistance.

again the focus has to be set at twenty-five or thirty feet, with a lens of about 250mm focal length on a 2¼″ square camera or one of around 200mm on a 35 mm camera; for good quality in the smaller format the image almost needs to fill the frame.

Opportunities also arise if the birds are swooping down towards some fixed point. While in Bangladesh we saw White-backed Vultures soaring high in the air above a marsh and guessed they were over a carcass of some kind. Driving towards the spot we came across a crowd of the birds feasting on a dead bullock, and others were joining them all the time. Placing

ourselves on a slight rise in the ground, we had splendid opportunities of photographing the vultures in flight as they swung down into the middle of the melée.

Taking photographs at the nest I have often set up two cameras side by side, one of them focused on the nest and the other on an area a little above it to get shots of the adults as they fly down on to it. This set-up and the results working at the nest of a pair of Montagu's Harriers are illustrated in the first chapter.

My attempts to obtain really sharp pictures that would show details of the wing movements of small

Above Swallow flying into the barn where it was nesting, photographed in 1949. The feet are completely covered by the stomach feathers to aid streamlining.

Opposite Four photographs taken by my son David with new high-speed flash equipment specially built for flight photography: *(left to right)* Marsh Tit, Robin, Wren, Tree Creeper.

birds in flight did not, of course, start with the invention of high-speed flash. The top speed of the early focal plane shutters was usually a rather dubious 1/1000th of a second, not nearly fast enough to show really fine detail in a small bird flying by. In 1930 I had an old Soho Reflex in which the shutter speed was adjusted by altering the width of the slit in the curtain, and I managed to close it down so as to obtain about 1/2000th. However, this meant working at large apertures since the plates of the day were so slow, and

satisfactory results were only obtained when photographing the larger birds.

Then during the 'thirties Harold Edgerton of the Massachusetts Institute of Technology developed the first electronic flash. This had a very short duration indeed and when some of the results arrived in Britain I got in touch with him immediately. We were exchanging letters when the war broke out and everything had to be postponed. Then in 1946, as related in the first chapter, the Dawe Instruments unit

Some of my earliest high-speed flash flight photographs, taken in 1947-8. *Above* Redstart flying in to perch, claws lowered and with the tail used as a rudder. In its bill it carries the larva of a rat-tailed maggot. *Right* Spotted Flycatcher hovering with a hover fly in its bill.

Opposite, above Cock Wheatear flying up to its nesting hole in a fallen tree with food in its bill. *Opposite, below* A cock Whinchat brakes as it prepares to alight.

became available and with the aid of Dr Henry's modifications and his photo-electric shutter release we obtained some of the first really satisfactory results. Cyril Newberry and I published the best of these pictures in *Birds in Action* (Collins, 1949) and it caused a small sensation. As well as photographing birds in the air we could now show the rapid aggressive reactions of birds or the drops of water being splashed by the wings of birds bathing.

Since those pioneering days electronic flash has

improved out of all recognition in terms of bulk, weight and reliability, but the flash duration has lengthened, making it difficult to obtain really sharp pictures with standard apparatus. To obtain the same definition and quality as when we started we have to use specially modified apparatus. This also has been described in the first chapter.

One of the bonuses that came out of using high-speed flash when photographing birds flying to their nests was that the food in the bills and talons was

Opposite Little Owl flying from its nesting hole, photographed in 1949 with high-speed flash and photo-electric shutter release.

Above A Sand Martin seems to fly towards its nesting hole in a sandy bank at almost suicidal speed. But in the last fraction of a second it brakes dramatically, turning itself into a parachute.

recorded so sharply and crisply that for the first time it could be positively identified. I have already mentioned the pictures of the Little Owls in this connection.

Positioning the photo-electric shutter release so that the bird will take its own photograph in uncontrolled conditions is a matter of careful observation. Just as people when coming home walk up the same road, through the gate and into the front door, so birds unless they are disturbed will usually return to the nest along the same route. A Great Tit for instance will often fly from the same bush and along the same flight path to the hole in the tree that contains its nest. By watching carefully, a place can be found where the release can be positioned. Alternatively the automatic release can be fixed just outside the nesting hole so that the bird takes its own picture as it flies in or out.

Some birds, such as the Dunnock and the Tree Creeper, do not fly directly to their nests but creep through the vegetation or round the tree trunk to reach it. So far I have not yet discovered any way in which these birds can be portrayed in flight in a completely wild and free state, so the following method has to be used.

The fine spread of wings of a Brahminy Kite photographed on the River Indus in Pakistan.

Members of the British Trust for Ornithology spend a great deal of time ringing birds so that they can be identified in the future. Sometimes this is done during the nesting season when the pullets are still in the nest, but for most of the year the birds are caught in almost invisible fine nylon mist nets set up along the side of a wood, between bushes or even in a reed bed. A lightweight ring with 'Brit. Mus. London' and a number stamped on it is fitted round the tarsus so that information about bird movement, migration, weight changes and parasites and other useful facts and figures can be obtained in the future. The bird is then ready to be released and this is where we come in.

Instead of the bird being released straight into the open we place it in a tunnel about twelve inches long, fitted with a cloth 'nurse's sleeve' at one end. The bird either runs or flies along the tunnel and launches itself into the air. As it flies away it cuts through the beam of light shining on the photo cell. This breaks a circuit and operates a powerful solenoid connected to the camera shutter, so that the bird takes its own portrait in full flight. This, anyway, is what it should do in theory but it is astonishing how often it manages to miss the beam or cut across it too low down or too high up, so that all we get is just part of the body. If we get one good result out of twelve we are doing well.

Mention has been made in the first chapter of some of the latest exciting developments in high-speed flash photography that David and I have been working on, and I am proud to include here some of his photographs.

The Cuckoo

Overleaf The adult male Cuckoo defends a territory like most other birds, and advertises his presence by calling from a conspicuous perch.

The Cuckoo is a mysterious and fascinating bird. Most people know that it lays its egg in the nest of another species. Not everyone knows that it tries to choose a nest of the species that reared it, so that there are Reed Warbler Cuckoos, Dunnock Cuckoos, Meadow Pipit Cuckoos, and so on. Altogether they lay their eggs in the nests of some fifty species.

The Cuckoo's egg usually resembles that of the fosterer in colour and appearance, apart from being slightly larger. There are exceptions: the eggs of the Dunnock, a very common fosterer, are pale blue but the Cuckoo lays an egg amongst them which appears totally different, having a creamish background with darker brown splashes.

Above and opposite A series of photographs showing how the newly-hatched Cuckoo ejects the eggs from its foster-parents' nest. In the first picture the young Cuckoo, which has hatched first, lies beside the eggs of the Tree Pipit. Manoeuvring its way under each egg in turn, and holding it in place in the hollow of its back with its two undeveloped wings, it works its way backwards up the side of the nest, continuing to push upwards until the egg rolls over the edge. In the last picture the Cuckoo, now alone in the nest, is fed by its foster-parent.

The European Cuckoo winters in Africa, its arrival in Britain traditionally heralding the real arrival of spring. We do not know how the young Cuckoo, leaving Britain some weeks after its parents in late summer or early autumn, manages to find its way to Africa.

In America the Cowbird behaves in much the same way as the European Cuckoo, except that the young instead of ejecting the eggs or the other chicks simply takes all the available food.

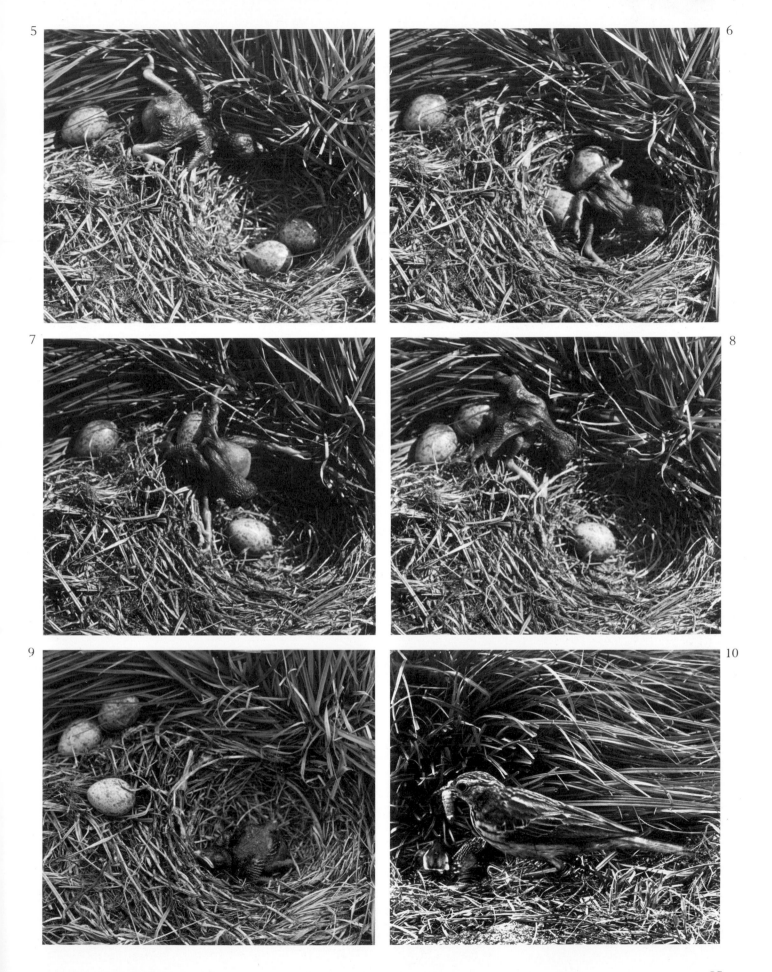

Opposite The persistent call of the young Cuckoo, which continues to beg for food after it has left the nest, appears to mesmerize birds other than its foster-parents. A Pied Wagtail arrives with food in its bill for the huge youngster *(above)* and *below* it is fed by a Meadow Pipit.

Above The adult Cuckoo photographed in South Africa. It seemed too tired to take any notice of my approach, and had probably just completed a migration flight. *Overleaf* In two or three weeks this fully-grown young Cuckoo will travel southwards to Africa.

Every time an egg or another nestling touches the sensitive hollow patch on the back of the blind fledgling Cuckoo during the first two or three days of its life, it is stimulated to eject it from the nest. It was a highlight of my career when I was able to take a sequence of this fascinating event in 1945.

The adult Cuckoo, however, having no nest of its own, is extremely difficult to photograph and it eluded me for thirty years. When I eventually succeeded it was only after eight hours spent in a hide with a recording. For some of this time the Cuckoo sat on top of the hide searching in vain for its rival, out of reach of my lens.

Ian Wyllie of the Monk's Wood Experimental Station has devoted a great deal of time and energy to studying the life cycle of the Cuckoo. On one occasion when we were visiting Monk's Wood, David was privileged to witness the spectacle of a Cuckoo laying its egg. Ian took him to a large meadow where he thought there might be some Meadow Pipits breeding.

As they approached the field they saw a hen Cuckoo flying up into a large tree. They watched her for some time as she appeared to make a series of dummy runs in the direction of the nest. In fact she was pinpointing its position. Then they saw her fly straight to the nest, deposit her egg, pick up one of the Meadow Pipit's and fly away. The whole incident was over in a few seconds and the Pipit probably did not know anything about it.

In 1946 I photographed an interesting series of experiments on the way different birds react to the Cuckoo. Working with the late Dr Stuart Smith and my friend George Edwards we found that a Willow Warbler would attack a stuffed Cuckoo violently. In general it seemed that birds like the Nightingale that resist a Cuckoo strongly are not often its victims, while the Dunnock, for instance, which showed little reaction, is a frequent fosterer. It was not a simple rule, however, for another common fosterer, the Reed Warbler, violently attacked a dummy Cuckoo placed next to its nest.

Monarchs of the Air

Above Lesser Spotted Eagle photographed during heavy rain from a pylon hide in a Bulgarian forest.

Overleaf The cock Marsh Harrier arrives at the nest with food in its talons.

Opposite A Golden Eagle at its eyrie on a cliff side in western Scotland, photographed in 1939.

Second only to the owls, the birds of prey have always been my favourites, and I have seized every chance to watch and photograph them both at home and abroad.

There is an interesting variety in the way the raptors hunt their prey. The Kestrel hovers in the air watching for a vole or mouse on the ground below. The harriers fly low over marshy land, systematically quartering the ground in the hope of diving at a Coot or a Moorhen before it reaches the safety of the reeds. A Sparrow Hawk will fly along a hedgerow and suddenly flip over

the top in the hope of surprising a bird feeding on the other side. The Osprey sweeps over water, hovering when it sees movement and then making a sudden plunge. If its prey is a large fish, it can have a great struggle to lift it clear and regain flight.

The splendid stoop of the Peregrine, appearing from nowhere and hurtling through the air at its prey, a pigeon maybe or a duck, has always excited admiration. I remember a conversation with Lord Alanbrooke just after the war. He had recently been on

Opposite The magnificent Lammergeier in its nesting cave in the south of Spain.

Above A 64-foot pylon hide had to be erected to photograph this Hobby making use of an old Carrion Crow's nest.

the Wexford slobs in Ireland when a Peregrine had suddenly appeared out of the mist, plunged like a rocket at a drake Teal, hit it hard and killed it instantly. The Peregrine rose, circled, came round again and without alighting picked up the Teal from where it had fallen and carried it off to a heather-covered rock to pluck and feed on it.

Not to be outdone, I told a story of a spectacular aerial food pass I had seen when photographing the Hobby from a tall pylon hide. The tiercel or cock had suddenly started to call as he flew by overhead. He was calling to the falcon but she was brooding over the

Above The Osprey calls vociferously from the nest as its mate flies past with a large fish in its talons.

Opposite, above Spanish Imperial Eagle with chick at its nest in the top of a stone pine tree in the Coto Doñana. This is one of the rarest birds in the world, with a population thought to be no more than fifty pairs.

young and at first ignored him. He persisted and kept coming round and I could see that he carried food in his talons, but the falcon expected him to bring it to the nest while he wanted her to come and fetch it. After some ten minutes the falcon's patience was exhausted and she leapt off the nest and flew towards the tiercel. Suddenly a Sky Lark appeared, whereupon the falcon immediately changed course, dived at the lark with great speed, missed it by only a few inches, swerved 'ound and tore after the cock. As the two met in what I thought was sure to be a crash both swung

sideways on, seemed to touch and parted. Although it was all too fast for me to see what was happening I realized that the tiercel had passed the food to the falcon in mid-air, for a moment later she was back on the nest with a Sand Martin gripped in her talons.

That great wildlife artist George Lodge was also present, and at Lord Alanbrooke's request he recorded both scenes in two marvellous paintings.

We had tremendous difficulty building a pylon hide to photograph the rare Lesser Spotted Eagle in its tree-top eyrie in Bulgaria in 1960. I shall never forget

Below A Griffon Vulture makes an aggressive display, mantling over the carcass of a red deer, in an attempt to keep other vultures away.

Opposite The White-bellied Sea Eagle, photographed in Bangladesh, taking flight from its perch.

Above A pair of Kites with young at their nest in a cork oak tree in southern Spain.

climbing up to the hide to take pictures and finding the nest empty and then seeing the tiny chick apparently dead on the ground below. A gale had been blowing and either this or the sudden departure of the adults from the nest had caused it to fall overboard. Though it was quite cold and lifeless, I put it inside my shirt to restore some warmth; presently it kicked, opened its eyes and became lively. By careful efforts it was restored to the nest and a quarter of an hour later the female eagle returned and settled down to brood the nestling. I then managed to take photographs despite pouring rain and appalling lighting conditions.

Opposite The Peregrine Falcon is beginning to recover from its precarious status of a few years ago. Pesticides working up through the food chain caused mortality and produced infertile and thin-shelled eggs.

Above The American Kestrel, a beautiful small falcon. Both these studio portraits were taken at Phillip Glasier's Falconry Centre at Newent, Gloucestershire.

The Lammergeier, half vulture, half eagle, is probably the most impressive bird in the world. With a nine-foot wing span, it has been seen at 25,000 feet. Normally a scavenger living on offal, carrion and bones, it will often drop the latter from a great height to get at the marrow—hence its nickname of Bone-breaker. It has been known to sweep a wild goat off a ledge to its death and sometimes attacks wounded animals, but normally it avoids living creatures. I went to Spain to try to photograph one and my first sight of the bird was unforgettable. The throat and breast are

bright orange, the head creamy and the eye orange-red. As we watched it flew into a small cave in a cliff-face. We climbed the mountain with great difficulty to find a chick nearly as big as a Turkey. The nearest possible place for a hide was 150 feet away, and even then I had to be roped to a rock. Staying in the hide for eleven hours, I obtained pictures using a 600mm lens of the Lammergeier carrying food to the nest in its talons. As the bird sailed by with its wing tip only two feet away, I was able for a moment to look it full in the eye. When we returned two days later we found a gale had

Above This Peregrine nesting on a Welsh cliff face was most attentive to its young.

Opposite In Pakistan falconry remains one of the favourite sports of the wealthy. Goshawks are still flown at the now rare Houbara Bustard.

blown the hide down into the valley far below.

Also in Spain, I took the first-ever photographs of the Spanish Imperial Eagle, of which probably not more than fifty pairs are left in the world. A nest had been found on top of a pine tree and we very slowly and cautiously built a pylon hide out of duralumin tubing, only working for an hour each morning so as to disturb the birds as little as possible. Once the hide was completed we waited for two days so that they would become used to it. Then I climbed up into it and waited. Eventually the eagle returned and after a twenty minute wait started to feed the chick on a rabbit. I then started to take pictures.

Vultures, like all birds of prey, have exceptionally keen eyesight. Soaring high above the ground, one bird spots a carcass and dives down, alighting some yards away and then making a stealthy approach to be sure the prey is dead. Its nearest neighbour, having seen it plunging, follows it down and in a kind of chain reaction other vultures appear from miles away. On one occasion, I saw a score of vultures eat the carcass of a deer completely in thirty-five minutes, so they have to get there fast. Sometimes they gorge themselves so much they cannot take off and have to regurgitate part of the meal before they can get airborne.

Falconers are a really dedicated race who keep their

Above A female Hen Harrier at its nest with two young, photographed in moorland on the Orkney Islands.

Opposite, above The lovely cock Montagu's Harrier taken with a 600mm lens in the Mara Masai Game Reserve in Kenya.

Opposite, below The Tawny Eagle is probably the commonest eagle in East Africa.

birds in immaculate condition so that they can perform at their best. The colour pictures of the Peregrine Falcon and the American Kestrel (pages 98 and 99) were both taken at the Falconry Centre at Newent in Gloustershire, run by Phillip Glasier who wrote the definitive work on *Falconry and Hawking* (London, 1978). The birds he showed us were perfect specimens and not a single feather seemed out of place.

To photograph the Peregrine in its eyrie (page 100) meant being lowered down a cliff face by ropes to a ledge two feet wide, the waves breaking sixty feet below. The ledge was so crammed with paraphernalia, not forgetting the photographer, that part of the hide hung over the edge. I knew when the Peregrine was returning by the clamour made by all the local gulls, but as soon as she alighted by the side of her downy chick, silence reigned.

The Montagu's Harrier used to breed in one or two places in England and Wales but has now disappeared; fortunately, it is reasonably common in parts of continental Europe. It is a migrant, and I will never forget in Kenya watching with John Karmali, that splendid wildlife photographer, several cock Montagu's Harriers

The flight silhouette of the White-tailed Eagle seen from below, typical of the birds of prey which are masters of soaring flight.

Two pictures of the Hen Harrier in flight over the Orkney moors. In the first photograph it is calling from the air before diving *(lower picture)* to attack an intruder to the nest.

Opposite The Buzzard starts to incubate as soon as the first egg is laid. Here the elder chick, already developing its feathers, can easily be distinguished from the younger.

quartering an area for food in the Mara Masai Reserve near the Tanzanian border. It was one morning soon after sunrise that we saw a beautiful cock alight on a bush and John skilfully manoeuvred the car into the best position for photography. I took a series of pictures using the car as a mobile hide, with the Olympus fitted with a 600mm lens moulded into a 'bean bag' (see page 159) resting on the half-open window. In many ways a car is an ideal hide because birds and mammals do not seem to associate it with humans and will often allow it to come close. Using the bean bag in this way you can adjust the height by raising or lowering the window until the camera is opposite your eye; this method is in many ways better than using a tripod when working with a lens of very long focal length.

In 1972 while staying with our friends Peter and Jennie Steyn in Rhodesia we were taken to the Matopos Mountains, a large range where several species of eagles nest. Val Gargett, who had spent a lifetime studying the Verreaux's or Black Eagle, asked us whether we would like to see an eyrie. It was November, when the birds were not nesting, and Val told us that the eaglet had flown from the nest a month before. Keen to see a typical eyrie, David and I started the climb, and as we stopped to recover our breath we saw a large brown and white bird fly to the nest. Val told us excitedly that it was the eaglet and

Opposite The rare sight of a family of Verreaux's or Black Eagles photographed in the Matopos Mountains of Rhodesia.

Above African Fish Eagle resting among reeds on Lake Jipe in southern Kenya.

suggested that David should hurry back to the car to get the Hasselblad and a 250mm lens so that we could get pictures of this fine youngster. There was a very old and dilapidated hide near the nest. We approached from the rear so that the eaglet could not see us, and as I crept inside and started to focus I heard the eaglet calling.

At that moment the cock Verreaux's landed on the nest carrying a dassie (rock hyrax) in his talons. The chick grabbed it from him, mantled over it and began pulling the prey to pieces. I could hardly believe my eyes. Neither bird took any notice of the noise of the shutter and then – was I dreaming? – the hen flew in and perched on a rock just to one side but still in the picture. I had only two films with me and both were used in no time. What a scene – cock, hen and fledged young altogether, and I had not been in the hide for ten minutes! I watched them for some time before the hen flew off, followed by the cock, but the eaglet was still eating the dassie when I left. Peter Steyn, who has probably photographed more African eagles than anyone else and who has spent hundreds of hours watching the Verreaux's Eagle, had never seen both cock and hen at the nest together. Just occasionally all the luck seems to come your way.

Mainly Wading Birds

Above Ruff and Kittlitz's Plover (right), spotted beside an isolated pool in the Wankie National Park, Rhodesia.

Opposite 'Wait and see': a Grey Plover which appeared in front of one of the permanent hides at the RSPB reserve at Minsmere.

Before the coming of the modern small-format single lens reflex with its battery of long-focus lenses, photography of the birds known as waders was extremely difficult. They are never still for more than a second or two except when they are sleeping. Most of their waking hours are spent feeding, probing continuously into the soft mud seeking their prey, the crabs, molluscs and worms. I used to attempt to photograph them with a quarter-plate (4¼″ x 3¼″) Soho Reflex fitted with an 18″ Tele-Tessar lens, the widest aperture of which was f6.3; to get an image of the bird of reasonable size on the focusing screen meant that even

with a lens of this focal length it had to be within about ten or fifteen feet. It was difficult enough to focus the bird sharply and to use a shutter speed fast enough to stop all movement but when the mirror flipped up and the focal plane shutter went off it made a noise like a cannon and the birds fled.

It was different photographing the birds crowding together before the advancing tide on Hilbre Island, that paradise for ornithologists in the Dee estuary. The noise made by the birds calling and quarrelling and the waves breaking completely drowned the noise of the Soho shutter.

Avocet *(opposite)* and Redshank *(above),* both photographed from a permanent hide at Minsmere. The Avocet is slowly walking through the shallow water. The Redshank had been preening and suddenly flapped its wings to unruffle its feathers.

After high tide, when the birds had settled down to sleep and felt safe since they were in the company of so many other birds, it was possible to use the old Sanderson Field Camera. There was plenty of time to focus carefully, stop down, set the shutter, put in the plate holder, pull out the slide and take a picture of the roosting birds. It was even possible to take a picture using the Sanderson's swing back to increase the depth of the field. It was by using this method that I took the photograph of the 5000 Knots all packed together (page 118).

But try to perform all these field camera movements with just a single bird that is feeding and long before the shutter can be released it has moved out of focus; even when using the reflex it was a daunting task.

I remember the difficulty of photographing a Little Stint seen at Rye Harbour on the Sussex coast in September 1953. Though the increasing number of birdwatchers has now revealed it to be a regular migrant, it was then thought to be a rarity, and I was anxious to get a picture. The bird was in continuous movement, first feeding in one pool then flying to another. I had with me a Contax rangefinder camera with a 135mm lens and almost every time I was about

Above Wood Sandpipers are not normally shy and will take little notice of a camera provided sudden movements are avoided.

Opposite Common Snipe, taken during a momentary pause in the constant movement of its search for food. A drop of water hangs from its bill which has been probing in and out of the mud.

to take a photograph it would move again.

The 6cm x 6cm and 35mm reflex cameras have changed everything because it is possible to focus right up to the moment of exposure. Lenses of 300mm, 400mm, 600mm, 800mm, 1000mm or even 2000mm in focal length can be used, provided you have a sufficiently rigid tripod, to secure photographs of medium sized birds thirty or more feet away. With fast colour film such as the 200 and 400 ASA Ektachrome, short exposures can be given that will stop all but the fastest movements.

The different species of wading birds have evolved different shapes and lengths of bill and feed at different depths in the mud, mainly on the larger invertebrates. Some that lie near the surface rely on a thick shell for protection, some hide under stones or weeds, while others live in burrows under the sand connected to the surface by a tube. Methods of feeding vary accordingly.

The Oystercatcher, which congregates in large flocks, has a thick, strong beak which it uses to chip through the shells of the larger bivalves such as mussels. Moving their bills rapidly up and down in the mud, they can hunt for food even on the darkest nights and when the moon is full the lovely trills of their call

Opposite Lapwings, generally shy and difficult to photograph, take no notice of the permanent hides at Minsmere and may come quite close.

Above In this photograph of a Common Snipe feeding at Minsmere the bill with its flexible ends can be seen partly open.

can be heard. The Turnstone, in smaller groups, turns over stones and weeds on the surface in its search for prey, but it can only prise open small shells. The Avocet has an up-turned bill which it sweeps to and fro under the surface of soft mud with a scything action.

I have often watched the Common Snipe probing the mud with its bill for minutes on end and wondered how many times it has to try before it catches anything. The tips of the bill are flexible and very sensitive. As soon as they touch some food the Snipe closes its bill, withdraws it from the mud and jerks its head to shake the food up towards its mouth. Its eyes are set a

long way back in the head so that it can keep a watch while feeding.

The Redshank has a straight bill and lives on a varied diet. Though it normally eats worms, crustaceans, bivalves, shrimps and small fish, it will also move into nearby fields when the tide is high and catch earthworms and leather-jackets. Old-time wildfowlers used to know the Redshank as the Sentinel of the Marsh, for it was always the first to become aware of the presence of danger and give the alarm call.

Many of my photographs of wading birds have been taken from hides placed where there was a good chance

Typical photographs showing the restless state of the birds as the tide advances at Hilbre Island in the Dee estuary in Cheshire. *Opposite* Sanderling, Redshank and Oystercatcher. The rock on which the birds are standing will soon be submerged. *Above* A pack of Knot in grey winter plumage (one bird still has the remains of its red breeding dress). Among them are a few Sanderling and (far right) a Turnstone.

of the birds passing by as they fed – what is called 'wait and see' photography. Sewage farms are often good places to choose and the foreman very often knows where the birds are likely to congregate. Some of the Royal Society for the Protection of Birds reserves have permanent hides and these can be very rewarding. Perhaps the best known of their reserves is at Minsmere, midway between Southwold and Aldeburgh on the Suffolk coast. I have spent many happy hours there photographing a great variety of birds from the tiny Little Stint to the tall Grey Heron.

Herbert Axell, the Warden for some seventeen years, has a remarkably close knowledge of the conditions required by various birds for feeding and nesting. At Minsmere, he created the finest reserve there is anywhere in the British Isles and one that is amongst the best four or five in Europe.

Supplementing his small full-time staff with voluntary helpers, Bert built a series of artificial islands in this area of waste land. Now in some years up to a hundred Sandwich Terns breed on the islands, together with a number of other birds such as Avocets, Yellow

So little land is left exposed at times of exceptionally high tides at Hilbre that the birds are forced to pack closely together. There are some 5000 Knot in this picture.

By contrast, the more solitary Great Crested Grebe, photographed on the Norfolk Broads.

Opposite These Oystercatchers are still being disturbed by the rising tide at Hilbre Island, although two birds to the right of the picture are snatching a moment of sleep.

Wagtails, Ringed Plovers, Lapwings, Common and Little Terns and Black-headed Gulls.

One of the joys of sitting in a 'wait and see' hide at Minsmere is that you never know what species of birds will come within range. I remember once a relatively rare Grey Plover suddenly appearing out of the blue, driving away several Little Stints and starting to feed within five feet of the camera. It was obviously very hungry and had probably been on a migration journey, since it is normally quite a shy bird. It is the uncertainty that makes 'wait and see' photography so absorbing and it is essential to take plenty of film. Nothing at all

may happen for hours and then suddenly you are taking pictures as fast as possible.

It was at Minsmere and on nearby Havergate Island that Avocets bred again in 1947 after a century's absence from Britain as a breeding species. After the first year at Minsmere they did not return for some time, but they are now well established there: in 1970 fifteen pairs raised thirty-five young. I shall never forget the anticipation and sense of heavy responsibility with which I took the first photographs of Avocets breeding in Britain at Havergate in 1950. I can vividly recall the moment when the first chick appeared and

The Little Stint at Rye Harbour in 1953.

Crowned Plovers strutting to and fro by a lake in Kenya.

the cock jerking his head up and down with excitement at the sight of it. Avocets are devoted parents, each one taking its turn at incubation while the other remains constantly on the alert for predators.

Whenever I hear the name 'Lapwing' I have a momentary vision of flat marshes, cold piercing winds and a grey sky – not the best conditions for photography! Lapwings often migrate to Ireland during the winter but you cannot generalize about this any more than you can about so much bird behaviour: they are individualists, and Lapwings have been known to fly across the Atlantic. Extremely wary birds, they can be recognized a long way off when feeding by the way in which they make a short run and then stop, look and listen. Their courtship display consists of circling and diving in a ragged tumble, almost like a piece of paper fluttering down from the sky, and during the nesting season their lovely screaming 'peeweet' call echoes across the marshes and fields. They are not easy to photograph and great caution is needed when working in the hide.

Taking photographs from a hide on Hilbre is quite another matter since there is no timidity and, as the birds jostle for position in front of the advancing tide,

The rare Chestnut-banded Sand Plover at Lake Magadi in Kenya,
one of the only places in the world where it is to be found.

Above Shelduck, photographed at Minsmere.

Opposite Avocets, photographed for the first time breeding in Britain after an absence of more than a hundred years. *Above* The cock waits to incubate the eggs so that the female can go to feed. *Below* The parent helps the first chick to emerge from its shell.

you hardly know in what direction to point your camera. Perhaps only three or four feet in front of the hide there will be Dunlin and Knot, a little farther away groups of Sanderling, just as beautiful in their white, winter plumage as they are in their rusty red breeding dress. Down at the edge of the water Redshanks are still agitated, calling and running nervously from one place to another and sometimes even swimming between two rocks. The Oyster-catchers come next, also noisy and constantly on the move. However, somehow all these birds seem to know the moment of high tide and realize they will no longer be pushed back any more by the rising water; quite suddenly they all become quiet. The deafening din and tremendous movement ceases, they all become still, and turning their heads back over their scapulas they start to roost.

Sometimes the high equinox tides are made still higher by a drop in barometric pressure and an increase in wind speed. It is then that the birds find less and less

Opposite Hilbre Island: Knot and Redshank, with a few Dunlin and Sanderling, mostly watchful but some starting to roost. A wave of the advancing tide can be seen breaking next to the Oystercatchers beyond.

Above Immature Cormorant at Hilbre, straining forward in alert attitude. The Cormorant shares the habitat of the wading birds, although they usually keep their distance.

space on the small island of the Hilbre group known as the Little Eye, and the Knot in particular mass together so closely that further incoming birds are forced to land on the backs of those already there and have to push themselves between them. On occasions they have been jostled so close to the hide that I have been able to put a finger out from the bottom of the hide and tickle some of the birds. They do not seem to recognize the finger as being part of a human being – since they quite often peck at me, perhaps they mistake it for a large white worm!

It is absolutely vital that the photographer having taken his pictures should then stay in the hide until the tide has gone out for some distance and the birds are able to resume bathing, feeding and preening. Unfortunately many photographers lack the patience to do this; once they have made their exposure they get out of the hide and frighten the birds away. This has happened so often on Hilbre that the birds have become nervous and will sometimes spend the whole of the high tide period in flight, not daring to land. So the impatient few spoil it for the majority.

Oystercatchers flying to higher ground which the tide has not yet covered, at Hilbre. Flying just above them can be seen a Curlew and to the extreme left a Herring Gull.

Sea and birds in restless movement at Hilbre Island: Sanderling, Turnstone, Dunlin.

Being so familiar with the wading birds of Hilbre and Minsmere it is always pleasant when on travels abroad to encounter one that has migrated thousands of miles from Britain. In Rhodesia during a spell of dry weather, staying with Peter Steyn, we got into the habit of examining any pool we saw through binoculars. The water attracts birds as well as mammals and we would often see several different species drinking, feeding or bathing, sometimes together. We noticed some birds at quite a tiny pool and started to manoeuvre the car into a position that would give us the best lighting. As we stopped we saw a Ruff and by its side a little Kittlitz's Plover. Neither took any notice as we carefully pushed our lenses out of the window and took pictures (page 108).

Almost everywhere we have travelled we have come across waders. It was in Kenya, when we had stopped by a small lake to see what birds were present, that a party of Crowned Plovers alighted in front of me (page 120). At once they all started to call and run towards each other with an exaggerated strut. This went on for two or three minutes, and then they all took wing, flying to the other side of the lake and repeating the performance.

Also in Africa we photographed the Chestnut-banded Sand Plover (page 121), a great rarity throughout the world except for one place in which it is quite common. To see this most attractive little wader you have to go to Lake Magadi, a salt lake in Kenya. Apart from two or three other locations, it is found nowhere else in the world.

126

Colourful Birds and Zoo Photography

Preceding page The 'wire-tails' of the male Red Bird of Paradise contribute to one of the most extraordinary and colourful nuptial displays to be found among any of the birds of the world.

Opposite The Kingfisher, undoubtedly Britain's most beautiful bird, seen with a sand eel in its bill.

Above The delicately-coloured Hooded Pitta, one of a number of species of Pitta found in South-east Asia and Australia.

This chapter contains a collection of photographs of the more colourful or spectacular looking birds. The natural habitat of many of them is in the tops of trees in the tropical rain forests, where it is almost impossible to get near them. As a professional wildlife

Opposite The Grey-backed Coleto, a member of the starling family found in the Philippine Islands.

Above The Red and Yellow Barbets of Africa have a remarkable way of singing in duet, synchronizing so perfectly that it is almost impossible to detect when one stops and the other begins.

photographer I am frequently asked for such subjects, and though I would prefer to photograph them in a wild and free state, in practice they have to be photographed in zoos.

It is usually a waste of time trying to photograph birds in their cages since the difficulties of arranging suitable backgrounds and lighting, let alone the problems caused by bars and wire mesh, make it very unlikely that a usable result will be obtained. To photograph them successfully they have to be caught and released in a portable studio. While some zoos are perfectly willing to co-operate in this provided it is not

during the breeding season, others are wholly against it, maintaining that to catch and handle a bird causes it to mistrust you and that the traumatic experience is likely to prevent successful breeding. I can see both sides of the question and never urge a keeper to catch a bird if he is unwilling to do so, but I have never noticed any reduction in breeding success in the zoos where I have worked.

Our portable studio was built for us years ago by a skilled country carpenter, a real craftsman. It is a wonderful construction that when folded takes up a space only 33 x 33 x 12 inches, but which opens up to

Opposite The male Paradise Flycatcher, with almost fully grown young begging for food, photographed in Rhodesia.

Above The Black-throated Diver has a beauty all its own, with its grey, black and white plumage.

make a studio 6 foot long by 33 inches square simply by clipping together a series of wooden frames. The end farthest from the camera accommodates a variety of suitable backgrounds. We carry a portfolio of different types – mountains, trees, moorland, the coast – all painted with an airbrush. They are designed to appear rather indefinite and are slightly out of focus in the photographs, giving a realistic impression. We of course suit the background to the subject, not only selecting a suitable terrain but also choosing a tone that

Above The Plush-crested Jay of the South American continent is often kept in zoos where it seems to breed successfully.

Opposite The Blue-naped Mousebird, found in Africa, behaves much like a mouse, running up and down twigs and branches.

will contrast with that of the bird.

A few days before making our trip to the zoo, we will have visited some old woodland to collect lichen- or moss-covered branches of varying thickness and shape, the more gnarled and twisted the better since straight branches do not appear natural. One of these is firmly wedged about a foot or more in front of the background. For certain birds we use rocks instead.

The frame is now covered with a big sheet of muslin, rapidly attached by means of Velcro and zip fastenings. At the camera end there is a big 'nurse's sleeve' wide enough to take a man's body, and this is first of all wrapped around the keeper as he releases the

bird inside and then around the camera lens so that there is no way in which the bird can escape.

Lighting comes from three electronic flash heads connected to a Braun F700 power pack. One is directed towards the background to eliminate shadows cast on it by the bird from the other flashes. One is positioned at an angle of 45º to the subject and the third is placed on the other side and a little above to give top lighting and to soften the shadows. The lights are placed outside the studio so that the muslin acts as a diffuser to the lighting and birds do not strike them when flying.

The pictures are nearly always taken using a

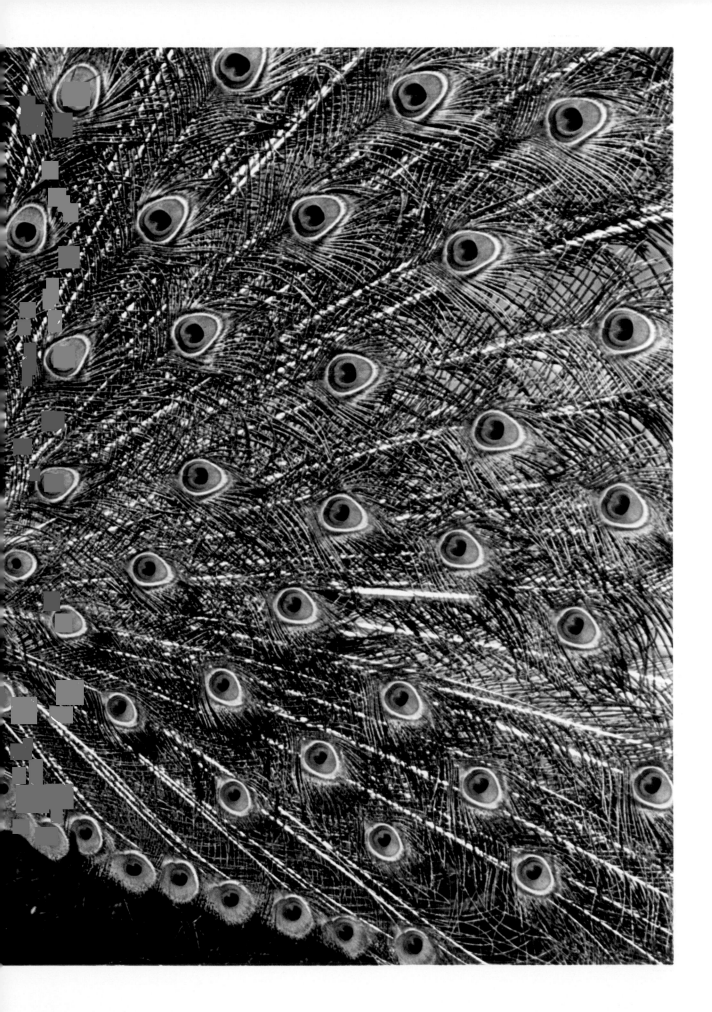

Preceding pages The gorgeous display of the Peacock needs no introduction. During the breeding season the 'eyes' in the plumage seem to have an almost hypnotic effect on the peahens.

Opposite The Jackson's Hornbill is found in suitable woodlands in East Africa. Its retiring nature makes it very difficult to photograph in the wild.

Right The Scarlet Ibis, brilliant scarlet all over, is found in Trinidad and parts of South America. Thanks to predation by man it is rapidly becoming an endangered species.

Hasselblad fitted with either a 150mm or a 250mm lens and an extension tube or a close-up lens. With Ektachrome 64 a stop midway between f11 and f16 is used when photographing average subjects, opening up to f11 if the bird is dark and closing down to f16 if it is light in tone. The flash duration is short enough to eliminate subject movement and camera shake while the stop gives sufficient depth of field without bringing the background into focus.

Everything is now ready to introduce the bird into the studio. We try to make sure no feather is out of place and then the keeper carefully places the bird inside through the 'nurse's sleeve'. It usually makes straight for the branch since it is the only place for it to perch. Occasionally a bird will take a little while to find it, flying from one end of the studio to the other. If instead of perching it settles on the floor or clings to the muslin for any length of time we very gently persuade it to move until finally it is in the right position.

The camera lens is slid slowly through the sleeve which is fixed around it and after that patience becomes the password to success: otherwise the bird may panic, becoming more and more difficult to

Above and opposite Some of the more colourful examples of zoo subjects photographed in the special portable studio: *this page* Virginian Cardinal, Toco Toucan; *opposite, left to right* Rothschild's Grackle, Superb Tanager, Cock-of-the-rock, Red-winged Parrot.

photograph. Once it has settled down on the perch it usually starts to preen or peck at the branch and it is possible to begin taking pictures, the bird usually paying not the slightest attention to the flash. After we have taken a series of front views, my assistant moves quietly around out of sight to the back of the studio and makes a gentle scraping noise; quite often the bird turns round to give a rear view. A slight sound made by drawing air through the lips usually makes it look over its shoulder at the camera and a different series of pictures can be taken.

In our portable studio we have photographed birds as small as waxbills and as large as eagles. The work is much harder than one might think because of the need to go out in search of new perches for each subject and keep up a supply of new backgrounds. However, seeing a perfect transparency makes all the effort seem well worth while.

East African Safari

Opposite The Black Heron mantles its wings to form a kind of umbrella when seeking its prey. Whether this is to mask reflections from the sky or to encourage fish to swim into the shade is not known. In the second picture a pelican swims past.

Above An assembly of White-necked Cormorants and White Pelicans at Lake Nakuru in Kenya.

Dorothy, David and I have been lucky enough to visit East Africa on several occasions, accompanying tours for Swans (Hellenic) Ltd. Although we have covered the same ground many times we have always seen something exciting and our cameras have worked hard. On average we have brought back some 3000 transparencies from each trip. Here is an account of a typical safari in this wildlife photographer's paradise.

Flying out at night, we arrive at Nairobi around eight in the morning. Our tour manager sees that the luggage of our twenty-eight fellow travellers passes through the customs and is loaded on to the minibuses that will be with us throughout the trip – thanks to him we can relax and are soon on our way to Lake Naivasha. From our first stop near the top of the Great Rift Valley we have a wonderful view of this extra-ordinary scar in the earth's crust stretching 4000 miles from the Taurus Mountains in Asia Minor right down to Mozambique. All the time we try to identify birds that to our companions are new and strange. Between Nairobi and Lake Naivasha we have counted up to seventy-three Augur Buzzards sitting on telegraph poles, starlings of several species, Red-billed Hornbills, Fiscal Shrikes, Black Kites, Ostriches, Ruppell's Griffon Vultures, Kori Bustards, Tawny Eagles – but I must stop for I know my enthusiasm runs away with me as my mind returns to those first African experiences. We have seen all these within a couple of hours of landing and wonder how many more we will encounter during the next twenty days since there are some 1500 species to be seen in East Africa alone.

After a two hour drive we reach the Lake Naivasha

143

Cattle Egrets stay near the wildebeest and zebras in the Ngorongoro Crater in Tanzania, ready to catch insects disturbed by their movement.

Hotel, set in the most wonderful grounds. Resplendent Superb Starlings, tamer than the sparrows in London, greet you and beg to be fed. Sacred Ibises search around picnic seats for crumbs, joined by unstriped ground squirrels, but both are beaten by a Hoopoe who drops from a tree, grabs the morsel and is away. Suddenly down by the lake comes the call of the Fish Eagle (see page 107), so typical of wild Africa – almost at once it is answered by another and the calls echo and re-echo across the water.

Faced with this feast of birds it is hard to decide if one should start with the easily seen and identified large birds or concentrate on the small ones. As we try to make up our minds a vivid flash of red and iridescent blue shoots by and every head turns to follow a Malachite Kingfisher. If we named the birds seen during the next hour or two it would be just a catalogue – one of our tourists listed nearly a hundred that were new to him on his first day. But dusk comes early so near the Equator and the heat of the day is replaced by chilling air; the sensible thing to do is to get to bed in good time to be ready for an early start.

Up until a few years ago the Lesser Flamingos on Lake Nakuru were one of the great ornithological sights of the world.

Immediately after breakfast we board a boat at the rickety landing stage and head out into the fresh waters of the lake. Untold thousands of birds come to feed. An African Darter perches on a dead tree trunk with its wings open to catch the sun – it is sometimes called an Anhinga or Snakebird, and when it swims with its body submerged and only its head and long neck showing it does look very like a snake. Our boatman takes us close to White-necked Cormorants sitting on their nests on dead trees. African Jacanas, sometimes called Lily-trotters, run along the broad leaves of the lotus or water lily, their very long toes spreading their weight so that they do not sink. Knob-billed Geese can also be seen amongst the water lilies, while a Purple Heron stalks through the dense papyrus.

Another species of kingfisher, the Pied, hovers over the water, suddenly dives and, coming to the surface with a small fish in its bill, lands on a branch and hammers the life out of it. Near the bank stands motionless the tallest heron in the world, the Goliath, patiently waiting for a frog or fish to reveal itself; two close relations, the Great White and the Little Egrets,

A Water Dikkop displays aggressively towards a monitor, partially
visible to the right of the picture.

fish nearby. The latter has an interesting way of
feeding, dashing and jumping this way and that with
slowly beating wings, looking rather like a ballet
dancer in its pure white plumage. It is stirring up the
water to make the aquatic life move so that it can be
seen and caught with a spear-like bill. The Black
Heron, by contrast, shades the water with its wings
spread out to form an umbrella. Whether this is to lure
the fish into the shade or to screen the surface of the
water from reflections is not known. As we return after
watching a vast number of species a final thrill is staged
for us – an Osprey falls out of the sky to catch a large

fish, struggling to lift it out of the water, not thirty
yards from the boat.

After lunch we go to Nakuru, the lake of the
flamingos. On my first visit in 1964 there were almost
a million Lesser and Greater Flamingos and from a
distance the lake appeared pink. Now there are fewer;
is the cause just part of a natural cycle or has the
pollution from the third largest town in Kenya killed
the algae on which these filter feeders depend? We
spend so much time watching and photographing
these beautiful birds that we almost forget the many
other species in this National Park. The water of the

Sacred Ibis in flight at Lake Naivasha, Kenya.

lake is saline due to evaporation, for there is no outlet, and consequently we find many birds different from the ones at Naivasha. On the latter were Pink-backed Pelicans but here we mostly find the White species. There are a lot of Yellow-billed Storks, African Spoonbills, Hottentot Teal and Cape Wigeon, while running amongst the legs of the flamingos are a number of Black-winged Stilts; nearer the shore Blacksmith Plovers are feeding.

We could spend many days here but our tour takes us across the Equator to Thomson Falls, a stop-over on the long drive to Samburu. Next day we continue towards Samburu, passing through Nanyuki and Isiolo, home of Joy Adamson's famous lioness Elsa, and reaching the game reserve in time for lunch.

Being so keen on birds I tend to forget about the mammals, but not here. To start with we see sixteen gerenuks, some standing on their hind legs to reach high into the acacia trees. The size of a mammal often determines the way in which it feeds, some browsing, some grazing, the giraffes feeding by pulling the leaves and branches from the tops of the trees while the gerenuks feed one storey lower; the impala feed on the stage below and the dik-dik near to the ground.

Above and opposite No series of photographs of African wildlife would be complete without two of the great cats: lion at sunset and leopard dozing in a tree.

We see quite a lot of elephants but none has long tusks. The ones that had have been killed by poachers and their ivory shipped to Hong Kong and similar places to be carved into ornaments to satisfy the tourist trade. It is an appalling tragedy that the largest of the world's land mammals should be destroyed, their tusks torn out and their huge bodies left to rot and feed the vultures. There seems to be no limit to man's utter selfishness; he has no thought for the future and does not care if his children, still less his children's children, never see a live elephant. His indifference to the suffer-ings of this noble beast, slowly dying in agony from hunger and thirst while a wire noose round its trunk or leg holds it in the blazing heat of the sun, is revolting.

Down by the river, the Uaso Nyiro, African crocodile bask while a herd of buffalo drink and wallow in the shallows; two very rare Grevy's zebras nervously approach, alarmed by even a puff of wind. But my mind is bird-orientated and my binoculars focus on a gorgeous Little Bee-eater behaving just like the British Spotted Flycatcher, flying up from a tree branch, catching some winged insect and returning to

the branch to eat it. Not far away a lovely Grey-headed Kingfisher preens its feathers in the shade, revealing vivid blue and dazzling red plumage. By the water's edge, among the crocodiles that are its favourite companions, a water dikkop spreads its wings in a fine threat display for our benefit. An Open-billed Stork and two Egyptian Geese fly down to quench their thirst; hosts of other species are seen and it is hard to return to the lodge without studying them all more closely.

But even at the lodge there is no respite, for Golden Palm Weavers and White-headed Buffalo Weavers come to take food from our hands! At dusk, Abyssinian Nightjars fly along the river and join with the bats in gorging themselves on the teeming insects.

Before breakfast next morning we see several Fan-tailed Ravens feeding on waste food from the restaurant while perched near the top of a tree a tiny Pygmy Falcon waits for a grasshopper to show itself. Across the river a Pale Chanting Goshawk prepares to hunt and other birds start to appear, but we have to set off for Nairobi by seven-thirty.

Above The cryptic coloration of the Two-banded Courser shown to good effect on the Serengeti plains of Tanzania.

A Rufous-naped Lark sings from the top of a bush in the Mara Masai Game Reserve in Kenya.

Knob-billed Goose among lotus and papyrus on Lake Naivasha, Kenya. The knob is exclusive to the male.

Our minibus driver knows his birds and slows down so we can watch a flock of Vulturine Guinea-fowl having a dust bath watched by a black-backed jackal and a couple of miles farther on he stops so that we can photograph a fine Blue-legged Somali Ostrich, quite a rarity. As we do so a small herd of reticulated giraffes passes sedately by. It is raining when we finally arrive at Naro Moru River Lodge but the bird life is still around us. A Hartlaub's Turaco flies by, showing his wonderful colouring of violet-blue, green stomach and brilliant crimson flight feathers, to be replaced by other lovely birds. Scarlet-chested Sunbirds visit equally brightly coloured flowers, three Cinnamon-chested Bee-eaters sit side by side on a branch while a Black Roughwing Swallow dashes by. We see White-eyed Slaty Flycatchers, Purple Grenadiers, Red-cheeked Cordon-bleus and Streaky Seed-eaters – what wonderful names they have!

Our next destination, Nairobi National Park, is close to the big town but even so there is a lot to see – kongoni feeding, an Ostrich family with the male in front, the female bringing up the rear and goodness only knows how many young in between hidden in the long grass. There are lions, including a pride of ten

The lovely Squacco Heron perches amongst floating reed next to a
water lotus on Lake Jipe in southern Kenya.

at the remains of a wildebeest kill, several herds of
common zebra and some common giraffes peering
down from their height of seventeen feet and not even
bothering to stop chewing the cud. Arriving at Athi
River we are met by black-faced vervet monkeys who
steal the food from our hands, but for the birdwatchers
the thrill lies in seeing two Peter's Finfoots swimming
along the river. Black Crakes with their bright yellow
bills and long pink legs search the undergrowth for
food and there are plenty of Arrow-marked Babblers.

Almost submerged, a hippopotamus floats in the water.
Pressing on, at Hunter's Lodge we add more exciting
birds to our list – a Broad-billed Roller sits in full view
for all to admire and on a branch just above the water
perches a superb Giant Kingfisher.

The largest reserve in Kenya is Tsavo National Park
which stretches over 8000 square miles, and no sooner
do we pass through the gates than we come across four
small herds of elephants standing in the shade of the
baobab trees – the poachers must have been at work in

152

The Purple Heron is remarkably difficult to spot as it moves through the reed beds on Lake Jipe.

spite of spotter aircraft patrols for none of them has large tusks. European Rollers are everywhere, Isabelline Wheatears are common and we see several glorious Golden Pipits. There are so many different species that we cannot stop to identify them all but before we reach Kilaguni Safari Lodge we get excellent sightings of a Long-toed Lapwing and a Blackhead Plover, both new to us.

Every game lodge has some special feature and here on the verandah we fed D'Arnaud's Barbets, Red-billed Hornbills, White-headed Buffalo Weavers and other species while unstriped ground squirrels even helped themselves from our tables. Marabou Storks waited for their share and down at the pools there was an ever-changing scene as elephants sucked water into their trunks, the warthogs enjoyed a mud bath, herds of common zebra stood warily, ready to stampede away, and impala, waterbuck, Thomson's and Grant's gazelles came and went. Scores of Little Swifts had built their nests on the underside of the roof, and African agama

Opposite The Hammerkop *(above)* is a close relative of the heron family. *Below* An African Darter or Snakebird perched on a tree stump on Lake Naivasha.

The Kori Bustard is commonly seen in the vast Serengeti plains of Tanzania.

Fulvous Tree Ducks walk through a small flock of White-faced Tree Ducks on Lake Jipe.

lizards with yellow heads, pink backs and undersides and bright blue legs and tails scavenged about.

On a 'game run' next day there is really too much to take in. A Bearded Woodpecker, a male with bright red nape, hammers into a rotten tree trunk to extract a wood boring beetle; a pair of Scimitar-billed Wood Hoopoes consider nesting in a yellow fever tree and a fine Paradise Whydah loops its way between the bushes. Already on the safari we have seen several Lilac-breasted Rollers but here we see the much rarer Lilac-throated Roller which is so easy to miss. Some of our party are lucky enough to see four Lesser Kudus, but some gremlin always prevents me from seeing them.

Leaving Tsavo next morning by way of Mzima Springs, where Alan and Joan Root made that wonderful film of hippopotamus and crocodile under water, we watch Royal or Golden-breasted Starlings in their dazzling plumage flying down to drink and see three species of bustard – Kori, White-bellied and Black-bellied – while a Crowned Eagle poses on a low branch; by the flies gathered below we guess she has just killed and fed, perhaps on an African hare or dik-dik. As we leave the park we spot the wonderfully named Bare-faced Go-away-bird, a member of the turaco family.

Speeding towards Amboseli Game Reserve we could see Kilimanjaro, at 19,340 feet Africa's highest

The kingfishers are one of the most brightly coloured families of birds in the world. Here are three East African examples: Malachite *(top left)*, Pied *(right)* and Grey-headed *(above)*.

Opposite The Speke's Weaver *(above)*, named after the Victorian explorer John Speke, is one of a very numerous family of African species which weave their nests out of vegetable material. *Below* An African Spoonbill preens its back feathers with its great spatula bill.

mountain, and remembered that when it was first discovered the Royal Geographical Society refused to believe that there could be snow so close to the Equator. At Serena Lodge scraps had been placed on a rock outside the lounge and it was quickly covered with Taveta Golden Weavers, normally a rare species but common enough here. Marabous balanced uncertainly on the low trees.

A game run took us to a marsh where amongst a great variety of birds we saw Glossy, Hadada and Sacred Ibises, Long-toed Lapwings, Blacksmith and Crowned Plovers, Hammerkop, Squacco Herons, Great, Little and Cattle Egrets, Marsh and Wood Sandpipers, hundreds of Jacanas, Red-billed Ducks, Garganey,

Hottentot Teal, Black-winged Stilts, Curlew Sandpipers, Knot and Pygmy Geese. There were so many things to photograph I grudged the time needed to reload the cameras.

Next day as we left Amboseli we had a final thrill. A magnificent cheetah, now so rare, was running in and out of some bushes. Suddenly an African hare darted out of one and shot off at an amazing speed, but the cheetah was even faster and had caught it within thirty yards. The hare was then carried to the shade of a bush and eaten within sight of us all.

Bad roads and thick dust prevented us from seeing much on the way to the border between Kenya and Tanzania, where we experienced the usual customs

A Great White Egret stands at the top of a dead tree preparatory to roosting for the night.

The flightless Ostrich, the largest bird in the world, feeds on the African plain.

delay. It was 2.00 p.m. before we reached the Manyara National Park but once there amongst the wildlife everything changed and our spirits rose. Blue monkeys, some with young, watched us go by, a large savannah monitor darted along an almost dried up river bed, a Livingstone's Turaco in bright green plumage with red on the wings flew across our path and we almost drove smack into a herd of elephants! Three lions were sound asleep up a tree, trying to get away from the tsetse-flies who stay close to the ground. It was hard to tear ourselves away but we had to leave for

the Ngorongoro Crater. We kept climbing until we had reached nearly 8000 feet and could look down into the 100 square miles of the huge bowl below, the largest caldera in the world. Sleeping in a log cabin that night we were glad of a fire.

I could hardly wait for the morning to come so that I could go down to the crater and see some of the creatures I had read so much about. A Land Rover in four-wheel drive took us down a narrow, rutted track into another world. Getting close to the edge of the lake in the vehicle we took pictures, resting our long-

The Goliath Heron, the tallest member of this family, is common in many parts of Africa.

focus lenses on 'bean bags' – small cushions filled with dried beans which give a very steady support to the camera, or else shooting through the raised roof. The flamingos were not so crowded together as at Lake Nakuru and in some ways provided better pictures, with perfect reflections in the water. There were plenty of Spur-winged Geese, Open-billed and Saddle-billed Storks to be seen but a black rhinoceros with a small cub by her side seemed about to charge us so we moved off. A spotted hyaena and a black-backed jackal made towards something lying on the ground and

approaching cautiously we found three lionesses feasting on the carcass of a zebra.

As soon as the lions were satiated and moved away the hyaena and the jackal rushed in to grab a piece of the meat but the lions had not yet finished and came back to lie beside the carcass. However, there is no shade in the middle of the crater so the heat soon drove them to a pool to drink and at once the hyaena and jackal were back. Vultures circled overhead and we knew that once they came down nothing but a few bones would be left within a very few minutes.

The African Jacana is often known as the Lily-trotter from its habit of running across the lotus leaves when searching for its prey.

Serengeti we knew we could look forward to fresh adventures.

Millions of mammals move across the 5000 square miles of the Serengeti plains during their annual migration. Mile after mile of wildebeest, eland, the largest of the antelopes, topi, zebra, Thomson's and Grant's gazelles, all accompanied by their predators, the lions, leopards, cheetahs, wild dogs, spotted hyaenas and jackals – it was an extraordinary experience to drive across the green and park-like country. 'I spy a leopard!' called our driver and there it was asleep on a branch with its tail swinging below, too lazy even to open its eyes as we slowly approached. But the second car had creaky brakes and the sound caused the leopard to raise its eyelids – every camera shutter went off at

once! We spent the night in a thatched bungalow at Fort Ikoma, and the following day we were on our way back into Kenya to catch our homeward plane.

There is so much to see on safari, a feast for the bird enthusiast and so much more besides. In this chapter I have only been able to write about the birds and some of the mammals, and space has precluded illustrating more than a small proportion of them. There are also the plants, reptiles, amphibians and insects, including huge butterflies and moths. You must go on safari yourself to see all that East Africa has to offer. However, you will need to go soon, for even in the fourteen years that I have been visiting Africa dramatic changes have taken place for the worse.

Seychelles

Overleaf The endemic Seychelles Kestrel, the smallest *Falco* in the world, photographed on the island of Mahé.

Above Lesser Noddy chick, doomed to become one of Nature's casualties.

Opposite The White-tailed Tropicbird typically nests in the buttress of a tree.

How the Seychelles were ever reached by so many different species of birds is a mystery. Tiny specks of islands a thousand miles from the mainland, one can understand their being found by seabirds, but how did small landbirds, often no larger than a sparrow, ever reach them? Did they get a lift for part of the way on a piece of floating vegetation, which would have provided food as well as rest, or were they brought here by an exceptionally favourable wind from Mauritius? However it happened, the Seychelles are a bird photographer's paradise with no fewer than thirteen endemic species of landbirds.

Dorothy and I were accompanied on our expedition by Sdeuard and Heather Bisserôt, very skilled and experienced natural history photographers. We all worked together very happily. Dorothy and Heather took over all the domestic chores, going shopping in a dugout canoe powered by an outboard engine, searching for wild pineapples and even baking superb bread over an oil stove.

Some of the 700,000 Sooty Terns on Bird Island.

Opposite, below A Sooty Tern incubating its egg gives a threat display as I stand close to the nest.

A pair of the very rare Seychelles Brush Warblers, found on Cousin.

Having landed at Mahé we had a rough crossing by boat to Praslin (the air taxi was too small to take all our equipment) followed by a trip in a dugout canoe to Cousin. No sooner had we landed than I completely lost my heart to the Fairy Terns, beautiful white birds with huge black eyes which hovered above our heads, just as interested in us as we were in them.

The Seychelles Kestrel is the smallest *Falco* in the world. I had a unique opportunity to photograph one outside the nesting season, thanks to Jeff Watson, doing research in the Seychelles for the World Wildlife Fund. He had spent two years working on this bird and as a result could tell me exactly where a particular bird would come in to roost at precisely six-thirty every evening. I imagined I would only get a single picture, since the lighting conditions forced me to use electronic flash, but to my astonishment it ignored the flash completely.

The White-tailed Tropicbird, wonderfully graceful in flight, is like so many seabirds clumsy on land. It usually nests either close to the sea under the buttress of a tree or else under a rock or thick bush, but it also builds nests high up on a rock face inland from which it can dive straight into the air. The chick (page 170) is fed for eight weeks on large quantities of fish, often becoming twice as heavy as its parents in the process, and is then starved for a week until it reaches its flying weight, when hunger forces it to seek its own food.

Above The grey-brown Common Noddy.
Opposite The smaller, black Lesser Noddy in a typically crowded nesting colony, on the ICBP island of Cousin.

Like so many birds on remote islands the adult appeared tame enough until we got close, when we found it had a huge, razor-sharp bill.

Late April or early May brings the South-east Monsoon and over 700,000 Sooty Terns gather to breed on Bird Island, attracted by the vast shoals of fish, then at their richest in the shallow water surrounding the Seychelles. It is one of the most astonishing sights in the world, and the noise is indescribable. On the island they can breed in complete security, free from predators and until now

undisturbed by man. As a result they are so tame that as they incubate their eggs you can come close enough for them to peck at you.

The Seychelles Brush Warbler, a relation of the warblers found in Britain and the United States, was saved from extinction when the island of Cousin, the only place in the world where it can be found, was turned into a sanctuary by the International Council for Bird Preservation. Robbie Bresson, the ICBP Assistant Warden, is so close to the wildlife he protects that he was able to bring these shy, rare birds to within

The Seychelles Fody or Toq-toq perches on a bunch of bananas in the Warden's bungalow on Cousin Island.

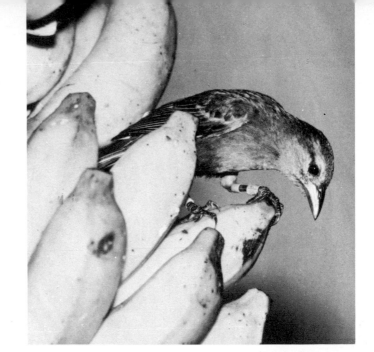

The Wedge-tailed Shearwater nests under rocks. Its weird call can make Cousin an eerie place to walk about in at night.

Opposite, above Female Black Paradise Flycatcher building a nest in a takamaka tree on La Digue.

Opposite, below The young White-tailed Tropicbird, first fed until bloated and too heavy for flight, is then left until hunger forces it to fly from the nest in search of food.

a few feet of us by imitating their call.

The Common Noddy, an attractive bird with grey-brown plumage and white head markings, usually nests in rock crevices close to the shore or else in the coconut palms. We often saw them on the foreshore gathering nesting material. A great deal of this was either blown away or stolen by neighbours, but the main purpose of this apparently fruitless activity is as a part of the nuptial ritual.

The Lesser Noddies, nesting on every available perch in the casuarina trees on Cousin, made almost as spectacular a sight as the crammed nesting colony of Sooty Terns on Bird Island. A single tree may hold several hundred nests and some 100,000 pairs breed on this one small island, with further large colonies on the island of Aride. The Lesser Noddy, often called the Black Noddy, is about half the size of the Common Noddy and darker in plumage. It also has a long, slender bill and a short tail which is very obvious in flight.

There are only some seventy pairs of the Black Paradise Flycatcher in the world, all on the island of La Digue. Jeff Watson, however, showed us three of their cup-shaped nests, made from entwined casuarina needles and straw. One held a chick, another was being built by a female (the male helps also), who was performing figure-of-eight weaving, and the third held a male taking his turn at incubating the single egg.

Opposite The beautiful cock Black Paradise Flycatcher has difficulty in accommodating its long tail feathers as it takes its turn at incubating the egg.

Above The Seychelles Bare-legged Scops Owl looks round as our tape recorder plays its call note.

Sparrow-sized, the male is unmistakable with its black plumage and long tail streamers; the female is quite different, lacking the streamers but with chestnut tail and wings, white breast and black head.

Another rare bird, the Seychelles Fody or Toq-toq, is so tame that it hopped about inside the Warden's bungalow where I photographed this one perched on some of our bananas. Once there were only some forty pairs in the world, confined to the islands of Frigate, Cousin and Cousine, but thanks to the ICBP there were over five hundred pairs by 1977.

Of all the birds we saw the shearwaters have the strangest life cycle. From the moment the fledgling leaves the nest in search of food it does not set foot on land again until it reaches maturity three or four years later, when it returns unerringly to the island of its birth after wandering thousands of miles. Two species breed in the Seychelles, the large, dark-coloured Wedge-tailed Shearwater and the smaller black and white Audubon's Shearwater with a rounded tail.

Because I have a passion for owls I suppose my favourite Seychelles bird was the spectacular Bare-

Above The hedgehog-like tenrec, introduced from Madagascar, is one of the few mammal species to be found in these oceanic islands.

Left The extremely rare Black Parrot photographed in difficult conditions, feeding high up in a bilimbi tree on Praslin, its only habitat in the world.

Following page The inquisitive Fairy Tern hovered only a foot or two above our heads when we landed on Cousin.

legged Scops Owl which is found in the mountains of the island of Mahé, perhaps on Praslin (though there is some doubt about this), and nowhere else in the whole world. No one has ever located a nest and very few people have ever seen the owl, but Jeff knew where to find them and, what is more, how to bring them to us.

Some time before he had managed to make a tape recording of their calls, and taking us to their territory he started to play it. The astonishing result was that this rare bird came to within three feet of us. Then occurred the kind of thing that makes photography so exciting and, occasionally, frustrating: A sudden heavy shower made me put the camera under cover and at that very moment the Scops Owl actually sat on top of the tape recorder searching for its rival.

Perhaps the most elusive bird in the Seychelles is the Black Parrot, which is actually coloured a dark greyish-brown. It is extremely rare and shy, having been shot by farmers over a long period because it ate their crops. A distant glimpse was the only reward of an afternoon's searching in the Vallée de Mai on Praslin, the Black Parrot's only haunt. Then early one moring we came across a group of them feeding high up on the ripe fruit of the bilimbi or cucumber tree; the dawn light was poor but I obtained this photo with a 600mm lens – it is not perfect but the circumstances would not allow better quality.

The dark blue, swallow-like Seychelles Cave

The first nesting colony of Seychelles Cave Swiftlets was only discovered in 1970, in a cave on La Digue. They use echo-sounding to locate their nests, grouped together on the cave roof in the darkness.

Below The lovely Fairy Tern with its single chick, which was hatched in a slight hollow on the bare branch. No attempt is made to build a nest.

Swiftlets, an endemic species, flit in and out of the caves in which they live like bats, the first nest only being discovered in 1970. Their metallic call, fascinating to hear, acts in the dark like an echo-sounder and lets them locate their own nest attached to the rocky cave roof.

I have mentioned that the first birds we saw when we landed on Cousin were the beautiful and fascinating white Fairy Terns, their big black eyes made to look even bigger by dark rings around them. They are tame and inquisitive and also slightly bizarre. For no obvious reason they lay their single egg on any tree branch or rock that has a tiny notch or crevice that might hold it. They do not use a shred of nesting material to keep the egg in place and consequently – and not surprisingly – very many fall to the ground, where they are promptly devoured by the skinks. When a chick is fortunate enough to hatch out nature has equipped it with huge, almost adult-sized feet with which it clings to its perch, literally for dear life.

Though the jets land three or four times a week in the Seychelles bringing people to enjoy the surfing and the lovely weather there is not yet hotel accommodation for a lot of visitors. Eventually roads and tourists must change things for the worse. Let us hope the Government will keep at least part of the Islands in a natural state so that the birds can live and breed in peace.

Galapagos

Overleaf The Galapagos Penguin, the only penguin found north of the Equator.

Above The Swallow-tailed Gull, calling in characteristic manner. It has the large eye of a nocturnal bird.

Opposite The protectively-coloured Lava Heron contrasts with the conspicuous red crab, which relies on its shell and the refuge of the sea to escape predators.

Apart from their interest to ornithologists, the Galapagos Islands must always be uniquely attractive to anyone interested in natural history. It was here in 1835 that Charles Darwin, voyaging in the Beagle, started the train of thought that was to result in the *Origin of Species*. Six hundred miles out in the Pacific off the coast of Ecuador, these small, volcanic islands that rose from the sea three million years ago were until recently remote, lonely and inaccessible. First

visited by man only four hundred years ago, they have a fauna which has evolved quite differently from that on the mainland, though it resembles it in many ways, and is still largely unafraid of man.

Not so long ago to mount an expedition to the Galapagos would have been a major undertaking, but the speed and comfort with which Dorothy, David and I went there was quite extraordinary. We had been invited by Lars Eric Linblad to accompany a party of

The Flightless Cormorant, tame in the presence of man like other Galapagos birds, is no more afraid of fellow inhabitants such as the marine iguana.

tourists as photographer-naturalists. After flying to Panama via New York and Miami, we boarded the appropriately named s.s. *Romantica,* a Greek liner that took us in four days to the rugged, rocky coast of the island of San Cristobal, where we anchored in Wreck Bay.

Next morning we visited the tiny Hood Island and were greeted by the Mockingbirds. At once I realized that things in the Galapagos were going to be different, since for the first time in my life I actually had to keep moving away from the birds in order to photograph them; they kept pulling at my shoelaces! The 'Hood Mockers', looking rather like a thrush, are distinguished from those on the other islands by their long, curved bills and more strident voices. As far as I could tell they were quite unafraid of man. The Small Ground Finches, resembling dark, dumpy sparrows, were plentiful as they are throughout most of the Galapagos and they are indeed the commonest of the land birds. Bright red crabs crawled over the black lava rocks of the low-lying island. The Cactus Finch, endemic to this small place, could be seen here and there, and the Galapagos Doves were numerous. The Blue-footed Boobies could be seen on almost every rock inland.

Galapagos Short-eared Owl. It feeds upon the petrels and shcarwaters that breed so commonly on some of the islands, and on rats and mice.

Lava Heron stalking its prey.

Unlike most doves and pigeons elsewhere in the world, the Galapagos Dove *(opposite, above)* is very tame, probably owing to its lack of enemies. The little Yellow Warbler *(opposite, below)* is found on almost all the islands, from the shore-line vegetation right up to the mountain tops.

Above The brown form of the Red-footed Booby (the other is white) perched in typical vegetation on Tower Island.

The Galapagos Hawk in flight *(above)* and standing on lava *(right)*.
The full adult plumage is almost black.

Waved Albatrosses pair for life. They share the incubation of the
single egg *(opposite, below)*. Often the sitting bird refuses to move
and has to be almost forcibly evicted by its mate, wanting to take its
turn *(opposite, above)*.

They are rather ridiculous-looking but very appealing
birds with large feet varying in colour from turquoise
through cobalt to violet. There was also a smaller
colony of Masked Boobies, dazzling white with black
wing tips.

The different species of boobies all feed by plunge-
diving into the sea after fish, but they do it in different
areas. The Blue-footed Booby can dive in very shallow
water near the beach and can even pick fish off the
surface; the Masked Booby works farther out to sea
but within the confines of the islands; and the Red-
footed Booby hunts well out at sea away from the land.
Accordingly, because their food supply is plentiful and

easily obtained, the Blue-footed Boobies raise two or
three young at a time while the Red-footed Booby,
whose food is harder to obtain, lays just a single egg.

The main attraction of this island, however, is the
colony of several thousand pairs of Waved Albatrosses,
the biggest birds in the Galapagos. They weigh
between seven and eleven pounds and are endemic to
Hood. Given a good wind they glide efficiently like all
albatrosses, but since conditions in the islands are
usually calm they have to take off by flapping and
waddling to a cliff edge before launching themselves
into the air.

On the beach we met a very friendly party of

Above The Waved Albatrosses have a most elaborate and rather lovely courtship ceremony, raising their heads and clappering their bills.

Opposite, above Galapagos Hawk in the pale plumage of the immature bird.

Opposite, below In contrast to the drabber coloration of the marine iguanas found on some of the other islands, those on Hood Island have handsome red markings.

Galapagos sea-lions and found everywhere on the black rocks of the sea cliffs marine iguanas which blended so well with their background that they were almost invisible. I also stalked the rare Galapagos Hawk, a large, very dark bird which preys on a wide variety of animals – rats, lizards, young iguanas – and on many birds, especially the doves and the finches.

At the end of our first day in the Galapagos, as the light started to fail and photography became difficult, we embarked in fast inflatable dinghies and had an exhilarating journey through the waves back to the air-conditioned cabins and superb food in the *Romantica.* What an extraordinary contrast it all was to the conditions we have experienced during some of our other expeditions!

Next we anchored off the island of Floreana and saw the beautiful pink Greater Flamingos in the lagoon Because they have been persecuted they are

Above A Hood Mockingbird hops from one rock to another.

Opposite A female Medium Tree Finch searches for food on Santa Cruz Island.

very shy and we had to view them from a distance. On the other hand White-cheeked Pintails and Black-winged Stilts, Turnstones, Whimbrels, Sanderlings and other birds were quite approachable. This is the only island on which the Medium Tree Finch is found. Just off the coast on the small islet of Champion we found the Charles Mockingbird, a dark species found only in this one small place. Floreana is also famous for the way in which mail is placed in a barrel at Post Office Bay and picked up by departing ships.

The climate of the islands is as erratic as it is unexpected. Though they lie on the Equator, they are surrounded by the relatively cold water brought north by the Humboldt Current and the climate is best called sub-tropical, though this depends greatly on the current's strength and direction. The warm season usually runs from January to April, the sky turning cloudy for the rest of the year. Rain falls at all seasons in the highlands but from time to time there is a very wet year caused by a warm current called 'El Niño', flowing south.

This climatic variation has a great effect on the numbers and distribution of the birds since they change their habitat in times of drought or heavy rain.

Above The spectacular display of the cock Great Frigatebird. Quivering his inflated red throat pouch, he reaches a pitch of excitement as a female sweeps by.

Opposite The pupil of the eye of the male Blue-footed Booby (on the left) is smaller than that of the female. The reason for this differentiation is not positively known.

Darwin's Finches, for instance, normally only breed in the rainy season from December to March, the first shower bringing a chorus of song from the males and a flurry of nest building. However, if there is no rain they do not breed at all while in wet years they breed all the year round. Accordingly a wet year brings a vast increase in the number of finches, even rare species becoming quite common, while a dry season has the reverse effect.

All the thirteen species of finch have their own special shape of bill, designed to deal efficiently with the various types of food on which they live. The large beak of the Large Ground Finch copes well with seeds: the long, thin one of the Warbler Finch can deal with insects. As no woodpeckers are to be found in these islands the niche has been filled by the Woodpecker Finch. However, it does not have the strong bill and powerful head movement of a real woodpecker. To obtain a grub concealed in a small hole it winkles it out with a cactus spine or a thin splinter. From a common ancestor these physical differences have evolved because of varying food and environment. It was perhaps

Above The Large Ground Finch, one of the many species of finches in the Galapagos whose slight differences helped give Darwin the clue to the theory of evolution.

Opposite The cock Blue-footed Booby displays to the female who is flying overhead.

the finches more than any other bird that developed the theory of evolution in Darwin's mind.

At Santa Cruz Island, measuring some twenty miles across, we visited the Charles Darwin Research Station sponsored by UNESCO, who are trying to save the famous Galapagos tortoises by breeding specimens from each of the islands in separate pens. In the past man has killed them for food while the dogs, cats and rats he introduced ate the eggs and the young. Facilities are offered to visiting research scientists and advice on conservation is given to the Ecuadorian Government, which owns the island.

Once again, the birds here were very tame. Stilts picked small animals from the mud of the salt lagoon with their long, thin bills, and Common Egrets, Great Blue Herons and Yellow Warblers could be seen close to the dwellings.

Throughout the islands you can come across amazingly unconcerned wildlife. On Tower Island I wanted to photograph a Short-eared Owl. Since it was in the shadow of a rock I asked Dorothy and David to persuade it out into the light; it looked at them in bewilderment and flew to within a few inches of my foot! The Flightless Cormorants, big birds with non-

Above Red-footed Boobies alighted on the rigging almost as soon as our ship docked by the island of Tower.

Opposite, below A Swallow-tailed Gull calls to his mate in mid flight.

Opposite, below The Red-billed Tropicbird has an almost fairy-like appearance in flight, with its bright bill and long white streamers.

functioning wings, simply ignored us. Elsewhere I fed a land iguana with flowers and the fruit of the opuntia, while Dorothy actually held a docile eight-pound marine iguana in her arms to be photographed.

Also on Tower we walked with difficulty across lava rock that was hollow underneath, the hollows holding 400,000 petrels that flew around us like a swarm of giant mosquitos. There were many frigate-birds or man o'war birds, the males with red throat pouches,

the females with white throats. On the ground the males looked like big red balloons as they inflated their pouches with their heads thrown back, making a trilling, gargling cry during the courtship display to entice the female to come down.

There are three predators amongst the landbirds, the Galapagos Hawk which hunts by day, the Barn Owl which hunts by night, and the Short-eared Owl which will hunt at almost any time. Man has ex-

Hood Mockingbird. The mockingbirds of different islands vary like the finches, each having developed a bill of a particular length or shape suited to the environment of the island.

terminated the endemic Hawk on San Cristobal and Floreana and it has almost gone from Santa Cruz, the Barn Owl is fairly scarce except on Fernandina, while the Short-eared Owl is not uncommon.

Conditions in the Galapagos are unique, quite different from anything we have experienced elsewhere. You have only to sit near the edge of a cliff in an updraught and if you keep quite still an amazing variety of birds will approach. Mockingbirds will sit on your knee, hop on your rucksack and play with your laces, you will see Red-billed Tropicbirds with their beautiful long tail streamers and Swallow-tailed Gulls and boobies will come quite near. In the water below sea-lions leap and pelicans stalk fish in the shallow water. It is a naturalist's heaven, and long may it remain so.

The Life of Birds

The courtship dance of a pair of Flightless Cormorants in the Galapagos Islands. The male drops a bouquet of seaweed in front of the female (1). Then he dances round her coming closer and closer until their necks intertwine (2-5).

Above and opposite Courtship display of the Slavonian Grebe. The hen flattens herself on the nest and stretches out her neck, while the cock swims round her flashing his golden ear tufts.

Every stage of a bird's life is fascinating to the ornithologist. Display, mating, egg-laying and incubation, the different ways in which the young are fed, the migration of some species – having observed and photographed birds for the whole of my life I still know little about them, for there is so much to learn.

The courtship behaviour of many birds is not easy to watch since it often takes place in trees or undergrowth. However, as mentioned previously, the birds in the Galapagos Islands are unusually tame. While we were there it was fascinating to watch the courtship dance of a pair of Flightless Cormorants. The cock returned to the chosen nesting site with a bouquet of seaweed which he dropped on the ground in front of the female. He did this several times and then started to dance around her, pattering his feet and coming closer and closer until their necks intertwined. After this ceremony had lasted for a little while the female adopted the mating position.

Different species of birds have their own particular type of courtship display. The hen Slavonian Grebe flattens herself out on the nest and stretches out her neck. The male, who has particularly brilliant golden ear tufts, swims round the nest, flashing his head from

198

The cock postures before the hen Black-headed Gull.

side to side and displaying to the hen before he approaches to mate.

In the case of the Black-headed Gull the cock adopts a variety of different poses in front of the hen. She will often beg to be fed and he may regurgitate food into her mouth as they are mating.

Crossbills usually nest in the tops of pine trees and continue their courtship behaviour during the period of incubation and while the young are small. The male collects pine cone seeds which he retains in his crop and as he approaches the nest through the branches the hen becomes more and more excited. She quivers her wings, opens her mouth and is fed before the young.

With some species a close relationship develops between the male and female and whenever the cock visits the nest he shows excitement and displays to the hen. I well remember once when photographing a pair of Great White Egrets in Hungary how each time the cock arrived he would call to his mate and put on a wonderful show, stretching his head forward and slowly flapping his wings. This occurred every time there was a change-over at the nest, for the cock helped with the nesting activities.

The hen begs to be fed.

They mate.

Preening after mating.

201

Above 'Courtship feeding' in Crossbills. The courtship behaviour, in which the female appeals for food from the male, still continues when there are young also begging to be fed.

Opposite, above A Great White Egret displays to his mate on returning to the nest. *Opposite, below* Little Egret bringing nesting material to the female.

The way in which nests are built varies from one species to another just as much as with any other activities. Little Egrets share the task but most of the actual construction is left to the female while the cock forages for building material. While he often finds a suitable twig on the ground, he occasionally picks up a branch that is too long and struggles furiously to carry it up to the nesting site, trying to force it through the foliage. If he fails he drops it and goes to find something smaller. Sometimes if there is no suitable material on the ground he manages to break off a twig from a

tree and brings the branch with the leaves attached to the nest.

After the nest is constructed the eggs are laid. Some birds will start to incubate as soon as the first or second egg has been laid. Others lay one egg each day and while they might cover them do not start proper incubation until the whole clutch has been completed. The Common Partridge is a good example of the latter. One of the most wonderful experiences I ever had was when sitting in a hide watching the hatching of a family of young partridges. Suddenly the hen left

Scenes in the family life of a pair of Common Partridges. The hen partridge returns to her nest.

As soon as the first chick had emerged, the female went off to fetch the cock.

The male returns, eager to see his first-born.

The chicks emerge one after the other once hatching has started, and as they gain strength the female stands up *(left)* to allow the strongest to crawl across to the male *(opposite),* who helps to dry them.

the nest and hurried off to fetch the cock. All the eggs were chipped and a chick was starting to push its way out.

There was a sound of running in the oats at the back of the hide and the hen returned, closely followed by the cock, who peeped into the nest and saw the first chick. Wild with excitement, he rushed about, banging himself against the tree beside which the nest stood, returning for another look and then dashing off again while the hen looked on. Eventually she settled down to brood but he continued to walk restlessly round and round the oak before settling down by the side of the hen. Some of the young then crawled over to him. After a few hours when all the chicks had hatched and gained strength, the cock called very softly. The hen moved away from the nest and both parents started to call the young to follow them. At first they would not come but another attempt followed and eventually a procession started through the undergrowth, first the cock, then the hen and finally thirteen chicks.

Many species of birds share the task of incubating the eggs and rearing the young. The Little Grebe is an example. I remember watching a cock once persuading his tiny chicks to climb on his back to be taken for

Above Little Grebe, with chicks embarking.

Opposite Hen Bittern shields her young from the heat of the sun.

their first swim. After he had paddled a few yards he suddenly dived with the two youngsters still on his back. A moment later they bobbed up again like corks while the cock surfaced a short distance away, returned and waited for them to climb aboard again.

While young Bitterns are very small the female stays at the nest to look after them, but since the cock does not help her she has to leave the nest when in search of food. This is a case where the male takes very little interest in family affairs.

Exactly the opposite is true of the Arctic Skuas: both parents are devoted to their offspring. While the hen keeps them warm the cock searches for food which he regurgitates either into the chicks' mouths or else on to the ground in front of them. During the nesting period the Arctic Skuas become very aggressive towards anyone approaching the nest – another bird, a fox, or a human being – and we have been attacked many times while trying to erect a hide or when entering and leaving it. The best way to avoid being struck is to hold a stick upright over your head so that they cannot dive at you, the same principle as that of a barrage balloon cable.

There are few more devoted parents than the Greenshanks. Through the kindness of Desmond Nethersole-Thompson I have had the pleasure of

Arctic Skuas of both sexes are devoted parents *(above)*. The male brings food to put into the mouth of his young, while the female incubates the remaining egg *(opposite, above)*. But the male drops the food. The female picks it up and gives it to the chick *(opposite, below)*.

photographing several pairs of these delightful birds. Greenshanks conceal their nests so carefully that they are one of the most difficult of all species to find, but they will often nest for year after year in the same place. Desmond, who has recently published his second monograph about them (Poyser, 1979), knew where they would be and from a hide only seven feet from a nest I was able to witness the hatching of the young. The empty egg shells can be very conspicuous, and soon after the chick emerged the adult picked up the shell, flew off with it, dropped it, and returned to the nest within a minute. Using an Olympus OM-2 camera with a motor drive I took a sequence showing the complete incident of the shell disposal, and three of the pictures are reproduced here (pages 210-11).

Birds use up so much energy in the course of living that they have to spend much of their time foraging for food, especially during the short hours of winter. The picture of an American Robin eating mulberries was taken at the Department of Ornithology at Cornell University from the laboratory of the late and famous Dr Arthur A. Allen. During the International Ornitho-

Opposite and above Soon after each chick hatches the Greenshank picks up the shell and flies off to drop it away from the nest so that it should not attract the attention of predators. This sequence was taken in the north of Scotland in 1976.

logical Congress there in 1962 he gave me a very warm welcome indeed and actually invited me to sit in his seat from which, through a window of optically flat glass, undistorted pictures of birds at the feeding table outside could be taken.

Many birds can be aggressive in competing with others at feeding places. We always put out food in our garden for wild birds during the winter, especially during very cold weather, and it is enchanting to watch the behaviour of the various birds that come to feed. A

tiny Blue Tit will have a go at a Great Tit or a Greenfinch if they come too near, and anyone who has been nipped by a Blue Tit knows how painful it can be. Small birds are often well able to take care of them-selves – look at the way in which the Robin becomes a ball of utter fury when others of the same species tres-pass on its ground.

The behaviour of Robins to each other is greatly affected by the way in which the colour of their feathers changes as they develop. The young Robin has

Opposite, above It is essential for survival that a bird's plumage should always be in good order, and many spare moments are devoted to preening and scratching to remove parasites or loose feathers. This very tame young Brown Pelican was photographed in the Galapagos Islands.

Opposite, below American Robin swallowing a mulberry, photographed from the observation post of Dr Arthur A. Allen at the Cornell Laboratory of Ornithology.

Above The 'pecking order' demonstrated by the Galapagos Mockingbird: the bird in the foreground cocks his tail, quivers his wings and opens his bill wide in a submissive display on the approach of a dominant bird.

Above Great Tit hurls defiance at Blue Tit at a garden feeding place.

Opposite Robin becomes a ball of fury defending its territory against a trespasser of the same species.

a brown speckled breast and after it leaves its parents and becomes independent can live in the territory of another, adult Robin because the bird does not recognize it as a potential rival. However, as soon as it develops adult plumage and grows red feathers on its breast even its parents will drive it away, looking on it not as one of their young but purely as an adversary. The young Robin then has to establish its own territory, trying to find an unoccupied area and perhaps taking over one from a bird that has died. Sometimes it will encroach a little on another Robin's property by force.

Whatever ground is chosen, it must supply enough food. If the adjoining territory belongs to a female Robin the two may link up provided the combined areas can supply sufficient to eat for the young as well as the adults.

In the autumn the female sings, like the cock; consequently she is driven away. Then in December her behaviour changes, she becomes submissive and is accepted by the cock.

While there is still much to learn about display, mating and feeding, the real mystery of the life of a bird lies in the field of migration. Most insectivorous

birds must migrate because of the shortage of insects in winter. But some Robins stay in Britain during the winter while others migrate quite long distances, in some cases even as far as Africa. A partial explanation for this might be that while there are sufficient insects in the winter to keep a few Robins alive there are not enough to feed all those who, having spent the summer in northern climes, migrate here in the autumn, bringing with them the young they have reared. Perhaps these northern Robins have evolved the habit of migration while those born in England have not. This is a plausible theory until we learn that from a single brood some of the young turn out to be migrants and some residents!

The major mystery, the way in which birds home so accurately across great distances, remains unsolved. Some Swallows that have been ringed in Britain spend our winter in the south-east corner of Africa, in Cape Province, the Orange Free State or the Transvaal. This means that their annual migration involves distances of up to 13,000 miles, yet individuals have returned each spring to the very same barn in which they were born, for periods of up to nine years. How do they do it, how do they find their way?

They cannot use landmarks since birds often migrate at night, many pass over very long stretches of ocean and birds that have been taken several hundreds of miles into completely unknown territory can still find their way home. The theory that they make use of the earth's magnetic field, having a form of compass inside their head, has been disproved. Old birds do not show young ones the way because some young ones migrate before their parents while others migrate after them; the young Golden Plovers in America, for instance, migrate 5000 miles from the north to the south by a quite different route from that taken by the older ones.

The problem of migration is a good example of the fascination of the life of birds; we really know so little about them in spite of all our research. So much work remains to be done, so many mysteries remain unsolved. For the photographer, however, first-hand observation of scenes in the lives of individual birds remains a constant source of fascination.

The Great Skua or Bonxie in full aggressive display as my companion approaches the hide to relieve me.

Appendix of photographic information

The cameras I used in the early days were the Sanderson Field (see first chapter), the Soho Reflex and the Brand 17. The latter was a lightweight, all-metal camera produced in the United States which had almost the same range of movements as the Sanderson but which could also be used in the hand. All these cameras were quarter-plate (4¼" x 3¼") in size, and were used with either glass plates or film packs (a number of thin sheets of film held in a metal container which were changed by pulling on a paper tag; they saved the weight and bulk of plate holders).

In the early days the material used was orthochromatic (not sensitive to red light) and I preferred Ilford's 'Golden Iso Zenith' plates. Later on in 1934 their 'Soft Gradation Pan' plate, which was sensitive to all colours, became available, and I used these together with Kodak's P800 plates, introduced in 1938, changing to their faster P1200 in 1946. The film packs were usually Kodak Super-XX but I also used Tri-X and Verichrome Pan.

In 1946 the Sashalite flash bulbs were replaced by the high-speed flash electronic unit with a flash duration of 1/5000th of a second and this has now been replaced by our Braun setup which gives a duration of 1/10,000th.

The Contax camera was fitted with a coupled rangefinder which worked with lenses up to 135mm in focal length; 'reflex housing' was used with longer lenses. When the Contarex appeared in 1963 I adopted this 'pentaprism reflex' with its range of superb lenses. The 35mm films I used were Kodak's Panatomic-X, Plus-X and Tri-X for black and white work and, for colour, Kodachrome.

Previously, just after the war, I had used 'Sheet Kodachrome' in quarter-plate size, but it had to be returned to the United States for processing; Kodachrome 25 was replaced by Kodachrome 2, and we also used Kodachrome 64, Ektachrome 200 and 400.

The Hasselblad outfit was acquired in 1970 to obtain 2¼" square transparencies, normally being used with 150mm and 250mm Zeiss Sonnar lenses and the 350mm and 500mm Tele-Tessars. Ektachrome film of various speeds was used.

Eventually we went over to colour transparency work entirely; if black and white prints are needed they are made from transparencies by making a negative.

Our 'Standard Zoo Technique' consists of using the Hasselblad with a 150mm Sonnar lens, with the addition of a 2M close-up lens. A Braun F700 flash unit is connected to three extension heads, giving a flash duration of about 1/2000th of a second. Using Ektachrome 64, a stop midway between f11 and f16 (f12.5) is normally used.

The Contarex outfit has been replaced by Olympus OM-1 and OM-2 cameras with a variety of Zuiko lenses of different focal lengths. The OM-2 has an 'automatic shutter' – the stop is set and the camera automatically uses the right shutter speed in most situations. There is an 'over-ride' which allows you to increase or decrease the automatic exposure in certain circumstances. This camera is used with an Olympus 'Auto-Quick 310' flash which gives the correct exposure without the need for Guide Numbers.

Key to abbreviations
S.G.Pan = Soft Gradation Pan
H.S.F. = High Speed Flash
Standard Zoo Technique = Hasselblad, 150mm Sonnar, Ektachrome 64, f12.5, Electronic Flash (three heads).
The technical information is given in the following order: camera, lens, film, f-stop, shutter speed or type of flash, location and date.

62 *Bittern* Brand 17, 21cm Tessar, Super-XX, f16, 1/10, Suffolk 1950

63 *Sanderling* Contarex, 250mm Sonnar, Tri-X, f5.6, 1/1000, Hilbre 1967

64 *Pack of Knot in flight* Contax, 135mm Sonnar, Tri-X, f4, 1/500, Hilbre 1949

65 *Great White Heron (colour)* Contarex, 250mm Sonnar, Kodachrome 2, f5.6, 1/500, Bangladesh 1967

66 *Herring Gull* Thornton-Pickard Reflex, 12″ Dallon, P1200, f5.6, 1/1000, Hilbre 1946

67 *Black-tailed Godwit* Contax, 135mm Sonnar, Pan-X, f5.6, 1/500, Holland 1952

68 *Arctic Tern (colour)* Contarex, 250mm Sonnar, Kodachrome 2, f5.6, 1/500, Norfolk 1964

69 *Dunlins (colour)* Contarex, 500mm Tele-Tessar, Kodachrome 2, f8, 1/250, Hilbre 1971

70 *Osprey* Leica, 400mm Questar, Pan-X, f8, 1/500, Connecticut 1962

71 *White-backed Vulture* Contarex, 400mm Novoflex, Pan-X, f5.6, 1/1000, Bangladesh 1966

72 *Masked Booby (colour)* Hasselblad, 250mm Sonnar, Ektachrome-X, f5.6, 1/500, Galapagos 1970

73 *Crowned Cranes (colour)* Hasselblad, 250mm Sonnar, Ektachrome 64, f5.6, 1/500, Tanzania 1973

74 *Common Gull* (two pictures) Contarex, 250mm Sonnar, Tri-X, f5.6, 1/1000, Shetlands 1968
Great Skua As above

75 *Heron* Contarex, 250mm Sonnar, Tri-X, f5.6, 1/1000, Norfolk 1967

76 *Swallow (colour)* Brand 17, 21cm Tessar, sheet Ektachrome, f16, H.S.F. Suffolk 1949

77 *Marsh Tit, Robin, Wren, Tree Creeper (four pictures, all colour)* Hasselblad, 150mm Sonnar and 2m Proxar close-up lens, Ektachrome 200, f16, H.S.F. 1/10,000 with infrared photoelectric shutter release, Hertfordshire 1978. Photos by David Hosking

78 *Redstart* Brand 17, 21cm Tessar, P1200, f32, H.S.F., Inverness-shire 1947
Spotted Flycatcher As above, but Suffolk 1948

79 *Wheatear* As above, Suffolk 1948
Whinchat As above, Suffolk 1948

80 *Little Owl (colour)* Brand 17, 21cm Tessar, sheet Ektachrome, f16, H.S.F., Suffolk 1949

81 *Sand Martin* (four pictures) As page 78

82 *Brahminy Kite* Contarex, 500mm MTO Mirror, Tri-X, f8, 1/500, Pakistan 1967

83 *Cuckoo* Hasselblad, 500mm Tele-Tessar, Plus-X, f8, 1/125, Suffolk 1970

84-85 *Cuckoos* Sanderson Field, 203mm Ektar, Super-XX, f11, 1/25, Suffolk 1945

86 *Young Cuckoo and Pied Wagtail* Soho Reflex, Ross Xpres lens, S.G.Pan, f4.5, 1/800, Suffolk 1936
Meadow Pipit and Young Cuckoo Sanderson Field, 21cm Tessar, Super-XX, f5.6, 1/250, Inverness-shire 1940

87 *Cuckoo* Contarex, 250mm Sonnar, Pan-X, f5.6, 1/125, Rhodesia 1964

88 *Young Cuckoo* Brand 17, 24cm Symmar, Super-XX, f5.6, 1/125, Sussex, 1950

89 *Marsh Harrier* Soho Reflex, 12″ Dallon, P1200, f5.6, 1/1000, Norfolk 1952

90 *Lesser Spotted Eagle* Brand 17, 21cm Tessar, Super-XX, f6.3, 1/4, Bulgaria 1960

91 *Golden Eagle* Sanderson Field, 12″ Dallon, Super-XX, f8, 1/125, Argyllshire 1939

92 *Lammergeier* Contax with reflex housing, 600mm Kilfitt Kilar, Pan-X, f5.6, 1/4, Spain 1959

93 *Hobby* Sanderson Field, 21cm Tessar, P800, f16, 1/25, Surrey 1946

94 *Osprey* As page 70

95 *Spanish Imperial Eagle* Brand 17, 21cm Tessar, Tri-X film pack, f35, 1/50, Spain 1957
Griffon Vulture at red deer carcass Brand 17, 21cm Tessar, Super-XX, f22, 1/25, Spain 1957

96 *White-bellied Sea Eagle* Contarex, 250mm Sonnar, Plus-X, f5.6, 1/1000, Bangladesh 1967

97 *Kite* Brand 17, 24cm Symmar, Super-XX, f16, 1/50, Spain 1950

98 *Peregrine Falcon (colour)* Standard Zoo Technique

99 *American Kestrel (colour)* Standard Zoo Technique

100 *Peregrine* Brand 17, 21cm Tessar, Super-XX, f11, 1/50, Wales 1953

101 *Pakistani falconer and Goshawk* Contarex, 50mm Planar, Pan-X, f8, 1/125, Pakistan 1966

102 *Hen Harrier and young (colour)* Sanderson Field, 21cm Tessar, sheet Kodachrome, f6.3, 1/25, Orkney 1946

103 *Montagu's Harrier (colour)* Olympus OM-2, 600mm Zuiko, Kodachrome 64, f6.5, 1/250, Kenya 1977
Tawny Eagle (colour) As above

104 *Buzzard* Sanderson Field, 21cm Tessar, Super-XX, f16, 1/25, Radnorshire 1938

105 *White-tailed Eagle* Contarex, 250mm Sonnar, Pan-X, f5.6, 1/500, Norway 1964
Hen Harrier (two pictures) Contax, 135mm Sonnar, Pan-X, f5.6, 1/1000, Orkney 1946

106 *Verreaux's Eagle (colour)* Hasselblad, 250mm Sonnar, Ektachrome-X, f5.6, 1/500, Rhodesia 1972

107 *African Fish Eagle (colour)* Hasselblad, 250mm Sonnar, Ektachrome 64, f5.6, 1/500, Kenya 1976

108 *Grey Plover* Contax with reflex housing, 300mm Kilfitt Kilar, Pan-X, f5.6, 1/250, Suffolk 1962

109 *Ruff & Kittlitz's Plover* Hasselblad, 250mm Sonnar, Plus-X, f5.6, 1/250, Rhodesia 1972

110 *Avocet (colour)* Hasselblad, 500mm Tele-Tessar, Ektachrome-X, f8, 1/125, Suffolk 1969

111 *Redshank (colour)* Contarex, 400mm Tele-Tessar, Kodachrome 64, f5.6, 1/250, Suffolk 1971

112 *Wood Sandpiper* Contarex, 1000mm MTO Mirror, Tri-X, f11, 1/250, Suffolk 1969

113 *Common Snipe (colour)* Hasselblad, 500mm Tele-Tessar, Ektachrome-X, f8, 1/125, Suffolk 1972

114 *Lapwing* Contarex, 250mm Sonnar, Pan-X, f5.6, 1/125, Suffolk 1963

115 *Common Snipe* As above

116 *Sanderling, Redshank and Oystercatcher (colour)* Olympus OM-2, 300mm Zuiko, Kodachrome 64, Automatic shutter, Cheshire 1976

117 *Knot, Sanderling and Turnstone (colour)* As above

118 *Knots* Brand 17, 21cm Tessar, P1200, f22 (swing back), 1/30, Cheshire 1949
Great Crested Grebe Contarex, 400mm Novoflex, Plus-X, f5.6, 1/250, Norfolk 1967

119 *Little Stint* Contax, 135mm Sonnar, Pan-X, f5.6, 1/250, Sussex 1953
Oystercatchers Sanderson Field, 21cm Tessar, P800, f11 (swing back), 1/125, Cheshire 1947

120 *Crowned Plovers (colour)* Olympus OM-2, 600mm Zuiko, Kodachrome 64, f6.5, 1/500, Kenya 1977

121 *Chestnut-banded Plover (colour)* As above

122 *Shelduck* Contarex, 250mm Sonnar, Pan-X, f5.6, 1/250, Suffolk 1963

123 *Avocets* Brand 17, 21cm Tessar, Super-XX, f16, 1/125, Suffolk 1950

124 *Redshank, Knot and Dunlin (colour)* Hasselblad, 250mm Sonnar, Ektachrome-X, f8, 1/250, Cheshire 1971

125 *Cormorant (colour)* Hasselblad, 500mm Tele-Tessar, Ektachrome-X, f8, 1/250, Cheshire 1972

126 *Oystercatchers* Contarex, 250mm Sonnar, Plus-X, f5.6, 1/1000, Cheshire 1969
Sanderling, Turnstone and Dunlin As above

127 *Red Bird of Paradise* Standard Zoo Technique (from transparency)

128 *Kingfisher (colour)* Hasselblad, 250mm Sonnar, Ektachrome 64, f8, two Braun 700 heads, Devon 1975

129 *Hooded Pitta (colour)* Standard Zoo Technique

130 *Grey-backed Coleto* Standard Zoo Technique (from transparency)

131 *Red & Yellow Barbet* Standard Zoo Technique (from transparency)

132 *Paradise Flycatcher (colour)* Hasselblad, 250mm Sonnar, Ektachrome-X, f8, electronic flash, Rhodesia 1972

133 *Black-throated Diver (colour)* Brand 17, 21cm Tessar, sheet Ektachrome, f11, 1/10, Inverness-shire 1947

134 *Plush-crested Jays* Standard Zoo Technique

135 *Blue-naped Mousebird* Standard Zoo Technique

136-7 *Peacock (colour)* Hasselblad, 250mm Sonnar, Ektachrome-X, f8, 1/125, Dorset 1969

138 *Jackson's Hornbill* Standard Zoo Technique (from transparency)

139 *Scarlet Ibis* As above

140 *Virginian Cardinal (colour)* Standard Zoo Technique
Toco Toucan (colour) As above

141 *Rothschild's Grackle (colour)* As above
Superb Tanager (colour) As above
Cock-of-the-Rock (colour) As above
Red-winged Parrot (colour) As above

Table of scentific and common names

The scientific names of all the birds mentioned in the book are given here, listed against the common names as they are used in the text and captions. Alternative common names are given in brackets, usually in cases where American usage differs from British.
As a guide we have followed, in most cases, *A Checklist of the Birds of the World,* by Edward S. Gruson (Times Books [USA] Collins [UK] 1976).

Common name	Scientific name
Abyssinian Nightjar	*Caprimulgus poliocephalus*
African Barn Owl *see* Barn Owl	
African Darter (Anhinga, Snake Bird)	*Anhinga rufa*
African Fish Eagle	*Haliaetus vocifer*
African Jacana (Lily Trotter)	*Actophilornis africana*
African Marsh Owl	*Asio capensis*
African Pochard	*Aythya erythropthalma*
African Spoonbill	*Platalea alba*
American Kestrel	*Falco sparverius*
American Robin	*Turdus migratorius*
Arctic Skua (Parasitic Jaeger)	*Stercorarius parasiticus*
Arctic Tern	*Sterna paradisaea*
Arrow-marked Babbler	*Turdoides jardinei*
Audubon's Shearwater	*Puffinus lherminieri*
Augur Buzzard	*Buteo rufofuscus*
Avocet	*Recurvirostra avosetta*
Bare-faced Go-away bird	*Corythaixoides personata*
Bare-legged Scops Owl, Seychelles	*Otus insularis*
Barn Owl	*Tyto alba*
Bearded woodpecker	*Thripias namaquus*
Bittern (Eurasian Bittern)	*Botaurus stellaris*
Black-bellied Bustard	*Eupodotis melanogaster*
Blackbird	*Turdus merula*
Black Crake, African	*Limnocorax flavirostra*
Black-headed Gull	*Larus ridibundis*
Blackhead Plover	*Vanellus tectus*
Black Heron	*Egetta ardesiaca*
Black Kite	*Milvus migrans*
Black Paradise Flycatcher	*Terpsiphone atrocaudata*
Black Parrot	*Coracopsis nigra*
Black Roughwing Swallow	*Psalidoprocne lalomelaena*
Blacksmith Plover	*Vanellus armatus*
Black-tailed Godwit	*Limosa limosa*
Black-throated Diver (Arctic Loon)	*Gavia arctica*
Black-winged Stilt	*Himantopus himantopus*
Blue-footed Booby	*Sula nebouxii*
Blue-legged Somali Ostrich *see* Ostrich	
Blue-naped Mousebird	*Colius macrourus*
Blue Tit	*Parus caeruleus*
Brahminy Kite	*Haliastur indus*
Broad-billed Roller	*Eurystomus orientalis*
Brown Pelican	*Pelecanus occidentalis*
Buzzard, Common	*Buteo buteo*
Cactus Ground Finch	*Geospiza scandens*
Carmine Bee-Eater	*Merops nubicus*
Carrion Crow	*Corvus corone*
Cattle Egret	*Bubulcus ibis*
Cape Wigeon	*Anas capensis*
Chaffinch	*Fringilla coelebs*
Charles Mockingbird (Galapagos Mockingbird)	*Nesomimus trifasciatus*
Chestnut-banded Sand Plover	*Charadrius pallidus*
Cinnamon-chested Bee-Eater	*Merops lafresnayii*
Cock-of-the-Rock	*Rupicola rupicola*
Common Egret *see* Little Egret	
Common Gull	*Larus canus*
Common Noddy (Brown Noddy)	*Anous stolidus*
Common Partridge (Grey Partridge)	*Perdix perdix*
Common Snipe	*Gallinago gallinago*
Common Tern	*Sterna hirundo*
Common Tree Creeper	*Certhia familiaris*
Coot	*Fulica atra*
Cormorant (Great Cormorant)	*Phalacrocorax carbo*
Cowbird (Brown-headed Cowbird)	*Melothrus ater*
Crossbill (Red Crossbill)	*Loxia curvirostra*
Crowned Crane	*Balearica pavonina*
Crowned Eagle	*Stephanoaetus coronatus*
Crowned Plover	*Stephanibyx coronatus*
Cuckoo	*Cuculus canorus*
Curlew (Eurasian Curlew)	*Numenius arquata*
Curlew Sandpiper	*Calidris ferruginea*
D'Arnaud's Barbet	*Trachyphonus darnaudii*
Dunlin	*Calidris alpinus*
Dunnock (Hedge Sparrow)	*Prunella modularis*
Eagle Owl (Great Eagle Owl)	*Bubo bubo*
Egyptian Goose	*Alopochen aegyptiaca*
European Roller *see* Roller	
Fairy Tern	*Sterna nereis*
Fan-tailed Raven	*Corvus rhipidurus*
Fiscal Shrike	*Lanius collaris*
Fish Eagle *see* African Fish Eagle	
Flightless Cormorant	*Nannopterum harrisi*
Fulmar (Northern Fulmar)	*Fulmarus glacialis*
Fulvous Tree Duck	*Dendrocygna bicolor*
Galapagos Dove	*Zenaida galapagoensis*
Galapagos Hawk	*Buteo galapagoenis*
Galapagos Penguin	*Spheniscus mendiculus*
Garganey	*Anas querquedula*
Giant Kingfisher	*Ceryle maxima*
Glossy Ibis	*Plegadis falcinellus*
Goliath Heron	*Ardea goliath*
Golden-breasted (Royal) Starling	*Spreo regius*
Golden Eagle	*Aquila chrysaetos*
Golden Palm Weaver	*Ploceus bojeri*
Golden Pipit	*Tmetothylacus tenellus*
Golden Plover (American)	*Pluvialis dominica*
Goshawk	*Accipiter gentilis*
Grasshopper Warbler	*Locustella naevia*
Great Black-backed Gull	*Larus marinus*
Great Blue Heron	*Ardea herodias*
Great Crested Grebe	*Podiceps cristatus*
Greater Flamingo	*Phoenicopterus ruber*
Great Frigatebird	*Fregata minor*
Great Horned Owl	*Bubo virginianus*
Great Skua ('Bonxie')	*Stercorarius skua*
Great Tit	*Parus major*
Great White Egret	*Egretta alba*
Greenfinch	*Carduelis chloris*
Greenshank	*Tringa nebularia*
Grey-backed Coleto (Bald Starling)	*Sarcops calvus*
Grey-headed Kingfisher	*Halcyon leucocephala*
Grey Heron	*Ardea cinerea*
Grey Plover (Black-bellied Plover)	*Pluvialis squatarola*
Griffon Vulture	*Gyps fulvus*
Hadada Ibis	*Bostrychia hagedash*
Hammerkop (Hammerhead Stork)	*Scopus umbretta*
Hartlaub's Turaco	*Tauraco hartlaubi*
Hen Harrier (Marsh Hawk)	*Circus cyaneus*
Herring Gull	*Larus argentatus*
Hobby	*Falco subbuteo*
Hood Mockingbird	*Nesomimus macdonaldi*
Hooded Pitta (Black-bellied Pitta)	*Pitta sordida*
Hoopoe	*Upupa epops*
Hottentot Teal	*Anas punctata*
Houbara Bustard	*Chlamydotis undulata*
House Sparrow	*Passer domesticus*
Isabelline Wheatear	*Oenanthe isabellina*
Imperial Eagle	*Aquila heliaca* (Spanish race *adalberti*)
Jacana *see* African Jacana	
Jackson's Hornbill	*Tockus jacksoni*
Jay (Eurasian Jay)	*Garrulus glandarius*
Kestrel (Lesser Kestrel)	*Falco naumanni*
Kingfisher, Common European	*Alcedo atthis*
Kite *see* Red Kite	
Kittlitz's Plover	*Charadrius pecuarius*
Knob-billed Goose	*Sarkidiornis melanotos*

Index

Numbers in italics refer to illustrations